"This book is a powerful guide to fearless living. Sue Patton Thoele teaches women how to honor, embrace, and claim their personal strength and inner wisdom."

—HEATHERASH AMARA, author of *Warrior Goddess Training*

"I am so thrilled Sue Patton Thoele has done a new meditation book! Her warm insight on strength, wisdom, and power is sure to resonate with every woman looking for support in these challenging times. I know I will keep her words by my side."

—MJ RYAN, author of *Attitudes of Gratitude* and *Radical Generosity*

"The strongest people in the world are women. It's our superpower. But we've been programmed to see ourselves as anything but. In *The Woman's Book of Strength*, Sue Patton Thoele doles out gentle daily doses of the medicine we need to meet ourselves, find ourselves, love ourselves, and encourage ourselves to grow into our innate feminine fullness. This is a superb deep soul writing and journaling companion."

—JANET CONNER, author of *Writing Down Your Soul, Soul Vows, Find Your Soul's Purpose* and many more

"*The Woman's Book of Strength* is like having a close friend and capable therapist at the ready, any time of day! This book is chock-full of thought-provoking quotes, meditations, helpful questions, encouragements, and simple practices to help readers access more courage, compassion, connection, and comfort. Think of any topic that supports us, stumps us, or brings us sorrow, and Sue Patton Thoele has addressed it in this wise and wonderful tome. Woven in throughout this book are her light-hearted, yet vulnerable, personal anecdotes that hold us in the warmth of 'you are not alone.' Want to feel more empowered and uplifted? This book is for you. Need cheering along the way? Sue Thoele is there for you!"

—SHERRY RICHERT BELUL, founder of
   Simply Celebrate and author of *Say It Now*

"This work IS the voice of a good friend reminding you of your deepest strength, your great capacity, and giving you the grace and permission to be present to the world as your truest self, without apology. Sue Thoele's lifetime commitment to women speaking up for themselves is an invitation to authenticity, living with intention and without regret. In this book, she becomes your advocate for living a magnificent, strong, rewarding life. Let her inspire you!"

—MARY ANNE RADMACHER, author
   of *Courage Doesn't Always Roar*

"In her lovely new book of meditations, Sue Patton Thoele urges women to 'use our gentle yet forceful power.' Heartbroken by the continuing rash of school shootings, Thoele gathers energy for a well of deep emotion, crafting a book for all ages. In beautifully written essays, each followed by action steps, her insights and suggestions guide readers to wake up to their inherent strength, wisdom, and compassion. Thoele aims to help 'women courageously claim and act from their inherent strength and gentle power.' The gorgeous result meets and exceeds her important goal."

 —NITA SWEENEY, award-winning author
  of *Depression Hates a Moving Target*

"Women of all ages will benefit from *The Woman's Book of Strength*. Its powerful message of women's inherent strength, wisdom, and grace is encouraging and exciting. Each inspiring meditation is an affirmation, a comforting guide reminding us to participate fully, to embrace our brave heart and daring spirit, and to share our gifts with others."

 —JUDY FORD, LICSW, author of *Wonderful Ways to Love a Child*

"Sue Thoele's book was just what I needed at this time. I found myself taking copious notes about her musings to utilize in my own life. The book is kind, gentle, and authentically from her heart. Among her many suggestions was HUG: Honor where you are, Utilize help that's available, and be Gentle with yourself. What can be simpler yet more to the point? And her reference to her 'holies' touched me deeply. We do all have them and to honor them, as she does, serves as a wonderful reminder to every reader to take notice. This book will change you and strengthen your hope in yourself and the world we inhabit."

—KAREN CASEY, author of *Each Day a New Beginning*

"This book is a powerful guide to fearless living. Sue Patton Thoele teaches women how to honor, embrace, and claim their personal strength and inner wisdom."

—HEATHERASH AMARA, author of
Warrior Goddess Training (edited)

"Sue Patton Thoele captured my attention and my heart on the very first page of her book *The Woman's Book of Strength: Meditations for Wisdom, Balance & Power* when she wrote 'When we are connected to our essence, women can create magic.' I believe it, and I also know that our essence often becomes clouded by fear, self-doubt, and other obstacles that separate us from ourselves. Patton Thoele's book is the antidote to that kind of separation. Thanks to Patton Thoele's gentle wisdom, guidance, and meditations—which are found throughout *The Woman's Book of Strength*—we can find our way back to our essence, our strength, and to ourselves to live in that space of authenticity where our hearts and our heads are integrated. *The Woman's Book of Strength* is a wise, powerful, encouraging book and with her writing, Patton Thoele reminds us we are too."

—POLLY CAMPBELL, author of *You Recharged: How to Beat Fatigue (Mostly) Amp Up Your Energy (Usually) and Enjoy Life Again (Always)* and host of the *Polly Campbell, Simply Said* podcast

The
Woman's
Book of
Strength

The
Woman's
Book of
Strength

Meditations for Wisdom, Balance & Power

SUE PATTON THOELE

Conari Press

Cover and Layout Design: Carmen Fortunato

For permission requests, please contact the publisher at:
Mango Publishing Group
2850 S Douglas Road, 4th Floor
Coral Gables, FL 33134 USA
info@mango.bz

For special orders, quantity sales, course adoptions and corporate sales, please email the publisher at sales@mango.bz. For trade and wholesale sales, please contact Ingram Publisher Services at customer.service@ingramcontent.com or +1.800.509.4887.

The Woman's Book of Strength: Meditations for Wisdom, Balance & Power

Library of Congress Cataloging-in-Publication Data: 2022932244
ISBN: (p) 978-1-64250-883-3 (e) 978-1-64250-884-0
BISAC: OCC014000, BODY, MIND & SPIRIT / New Thought

Printed in the United States of America

DEDICATED TO

Judith (Juju) Mangus, whose love, understanding, and knowing offer me safe harbor and mystical gateway.

Christie Coates, whose love of and commitment to spiritual connection inspire my own.

Mary Bell Nyman, teacher extraordinaire, whose light-hearted wisdom dances through these pages.

TABLE OF CONTENTS

INTRODUCTION

As my wise friend Pat says, "Women have always been the underlying strength." I agree. Unfortunately, while underlying is defined as *fundamental, basic, implicit, indispensable, crucial,* and *primary,* it's also described as *veiled* and *only discovered by close scrutiny or analysis.* For eons, and for many reasons, male-dominated societies have downplayed women's strength. In order to bring balance and harmony to our beleaguered world, now is the time to elevate feminine energy and strength—in both women and men— to the overarching position of responsibility and empowerment. Because feminine strength includes qualities such as respect, fairness, and inclusion, it needs to take it's rightful place in all echelons of society: home, business, education, physical and mental health, and politics to name a few.

Women are incredibly strong. Even under dire circumstances, most women are inherently able to overcome whatever life throws at them in order to accomplish what is needed in the moment. Along with a woman's ability to be strong is their capacity to do so without sacrificing the feminine qualities of wisdom, compassion, and empathy. Innately, women know how to balance strength with caring and respect. When we act from our hearts (which we often do), our strength is guided by kindness and sensitivity to the needs of both ourselves and others.

Women have a deep and holy hunger for equality and justice. At our strongest and best, we insist upon fairness and overcome divisiveness with understanding and compassion. With a gift for empathy, we also conscientiously search for solutions and options that work toward the highest good for all concerned.

Society desperately needs the tempering and respectful energy of feminine strength. Mass shootings break our hearts, stories of abused women and children haunt our dreams, and elitist disregard for the feelings and rights of the vulnerable leave us seething. With good reason, our hearts ache to make things better. Since our caring and passion run so deeply, what keeps us from acknowledging and acting from our unique strengths? Why are we hesitant to use our gentle yet forceful power?

Two major reasons: conditioning and fear.

THE HEART OF THE MATTER

The heart of the matter is that women have been conditioned to play small and modulate their strength and wisdom. We've been trained to hide our light and have had our influence and actions curtailed by laws and customs. No more! The Chinese proverb "When sleeping women wake, mountains move" is being affirmed by societal shifts throughout the world. We are awake and deeply aware that our strength, wisdom, and compassion are needed. For our world to survive—for Earth to remain a beautiful, bounteous, and healthy environment—and people to live happy, productive, and cooperative lives, feminine energy and strength *must* be acknowledged, honored, and empowered individually and globally.

LIFTING OUR VOICES

I write this a few weeks after a gunman killed ten people in a supermarket fifteen miles from my home. Another heartbreaking example of the world's desperate need for feminine qualities and values to have a greater voice in planning, power, and leading. A voice that understands basic human needs for safety, education, and mental and physical health. A voice whose heart advocates for the well-being of all. My prayer for *The Woman's Book of Strength: Meditations for Wisdom, Balance, and Power* is that it helps women courageously claim and act from their inherent strength and kind power. Feminine strength has been denigrated for ages, and that must end now. We are called to find, and use, our natural feminine gifts of inclusion, wisdom, civility, respect, and acceptance both privately and publicly. Women's gifts promote connection instead of separation, and build up rather than tear down.

It is my fervent hope that *The Woman's Book of Strength* helps women own their deep-seated strength so completely that no amount of bullying can make them doubt it or keep them from acting on it. The mighty and loving power of feminine strength is needed in order to civilize and humanize our dangerously out-of-balance world. It's up to us. We are the world's hope. And we can do it!

WHY THIS BOOK?

All my books begin in the fertile soil of my own growth, and *The Woman's Book of Strength* is no exception. It arose from a steaming pit of outrage. Infuriated by huge injustices in the world and smaller ones I dealt with personally, I stewed and seethed and resisted and blamed. Prompted by deep unrest and persistent spiritual nudges, the therapist in me eventually kicked in, and I realized I'd succumbed to old patterns of questioning my wisdom and giving away my personal power. Recognizing I was much angrier with myself than I was with "them," I could figure out why I'd lapsed into self-sabotaging behavior, forgive myself for doing so, and begin the process of owning up to (and acting from) my innate strength and power.

Because I have grown increasingly able to relate to myself and others from a place of sacred feminine strength, the last few years have been the happiest and most peaceful of my life. The same is true for many women I know who are on similar paths. Since those of us activating our strengths and owning our wisdom are laughing more, sleeping better, reveling in life, and kicking some butt along the way, I wanted to share the journey with you.

USING *THE WOMAN'S BOOK OF STRENGTH: MEDITATIONS FOR WISDOM, BALANCE, AND POWER*

This book is a compilation of bite-sized meditations, stories, and musings on becoming stronger, happier, healthier, and better able to have a positive impact in all areas of your personal and public life. Accepting, honoring, and activating our unique strength and wisdom facilitates positive change within us and encourages (or demands, if need be) the world to become a better place.

Please use *The Woman's Book of Strength* in ways that feed your soul. That may be reading it cover to cover, having it as a bathroom buddy, choosing topics from the table of contents, or asking a question and opening it at random. Whatever works for you. No matter how you are inspired to play with it, I hope *The Woman's Book of Strength* becomes your ally and that you can hear me cheering you on as you courageously, compassionately, and *gently* become stronger and more empowered. I also hope *Strength* makes you chuckle on occasion.

1

DEEPENING CONNECTION

*Only through our connectedness to others can we really know
and enhance the self. And only through working on the self
can we begin to enhance our connectedness to others.*

—HARRIET LERNER

When we are connected to our essence, women can create magic. And our mystical heart-centered—yet extremely practical—strength is urgently needed now to right a world disastrously out of balance.

Many women I know have had enough of heartless imbalance, inequality, righteous meanness, and downright disgusting behavior, and are committed to connecting with their feminine power and flooding the weary world with its constructive energy. To truly right the wrongs, privately and publicly, we must embrace the heartfelt feminine strengths of inclusivity, compassion, fairness, understanding, and the ability to be present and listen.

As women, we have a deep and holy hunger to be connected to our authentic selves and to the hearts of others. We long to live in a world filled with balance, harmony, and happiness. For this to happen, *head* and *heart* energy must integrate and equalize. Because feminine wisdom understands and embodies heart qualities, we are the ones who can bring that crucial balance to fruition, and we are. Only when heart and mind complement each other will equal pay, equal say, and complete respect for all become reality.

FACING FEAR

One of the hardest things I've ever done is come face to face with how incessantly fear ruled my life. Love connects us to self and others and fear divides us. I believe all feelings and philosophies are on a continuum between love and fear, and for the first few decades of my life, I hung out at the fear end. Since babies are born more curious than fearful, how did I get to be such a scaredy cat? Partially, I was taught to be fearful, but mainly I absorbed it energetically from the circumstances and people around me. I was born on the only day that week my dad had found work, money was tighter than today's jeans, and war was on the horizon. With good reason, uncertainty was rampant.

Sounds familiar, doesn't it? Society is once again in a time of transition, and it is not an easy one. Domination and imbalance need to change—in self, society, community, business, and home—and dominating people in entitled positions are not going to make that easy. However, facing and moving through fear will help us have the strength to bring about fairness, equality, and freedom for ourselves and others.

The first step is to courageously face our fears. Everyone has fear. The faces of fear change as we journey through life, but one thing is undeniably true: *unexamined* fear has the upper hand. *Unacknowledged* fear weakens, diminishes, and silences us. *Hidden* fear dampens happiness and hobbles us to self-sabotaging behaviors. Let's *dis*empower fear by gently becoming aware of it.

During your day…

- ✧ With no judgment, courageously begin to notice big and little fears.
- ✧ If you think you don't have any fear, tenderly dig a little deeper.

> *The fears we don't face become our limitations.*
> —ROBIN SHARMA

COMPLETING THE MOTHER CIRCLE

My in-a-nutshell definition of completing the mother circle is accepting the mothering you received, no matter its quality, and then becoming your own *good mother*. My years in private psychotherapy practice affirmed my belief that a troubled relationship with her mother can become a woman's most profound trigger. Because of the intense feelings involved, reaching acceptance for such a relationship often takes a tremendous amount of strength and patience. If your childhood wounds are deep and longstanding, please be kind to yourself and seek professional help. A compassionate and skillful therapist, counselor, or clergy person can help you weather the intense emotional storms that often accompany working through mother issues. From a neutral point of view, a therapist can provide valuable insight and perspective as well as practical tools to help you move toward acceptance.

Steps toward acceptance often include speaking your truth in safe ways and places, understanding Mom better by putting yourself in her shoes, and practicing forgiveness. Although we can't change the past, with healing, intention, and understanding, we can become better mothers to our kids and supportive and loving mothers to ourselves.

If your mother was/is a dear friend and supporter, your main challenge may be accepting the idea of her death. I was blessed to have a strong, loving mother. Even so, I didn't come full circle in our relationship until she was terminally ill and allowed me to really *see* her. Mother was a great support to me, but I hadn't known she needed my support also. Impending death gave her permission to be vulnerable and authentic with me, and I came to really *know* her. With that intimate two-way connection, we completed our circle by forgiving the hard parts and openly expressing our love and gratitude to each other for the rest. Of course, that sweet completion makes me miss her even more deeply.

During your day...

- ✧ With deep compassion, note any unfinished business between you and your mother.
- ✧ In the theater of your mind, view a scene between you and your mom. With the magic of imagination, put yourself in her shoes. What is she feeling? What is she afraid of? What are her intentions? Give her a little blessing and let her image fade.
- ✧ Allow your attention to return to you in the scene and gently give yourself what you want, need, and deserve.

> *Forgiving unskillful mothering and creating an internal good mother facilitate the ability to claim your own feminine strength, wisdom, and power.*

RECLAIMING YOUR SELVES

To deepen our connection with ourselves, it's important to know that we are many individual personas housed in one body. Each of us has a varied cast of characters that make up our personality. One moment a great businesswoman, the next someone entirely different. In Transpersonal Psychology, these varied facets are referred to as *subpersonalities*. The two best metaphors I've found to explain subpersonalities are a *symphony orchestra* and a *stage play*. Let's start there.

The stage play

Subpersonality	Part an actor plays	Aspects of ourselves that interact with the world and those in it.
The **I**	Director of the play	Objective decision maker, discerner, and choice maker.
Higher Self	Playwright	Creator of the play. Connected to intuition, wisdom, and the Divine. Always has our best interest at heart. Sees the whole picture.

The symphony orchestra

Subpersonalities	Individual instruments
The **I**	Conductor
Higher Self	Composer

For us to be strong, successful, and happy, our inner cast needs to cooperate and complement each other just as an acting ensemble and orchestra members do in a performance. Although some of us were trained to deny or diminish our strong feminine aspects to appease others, they are still with us waiting to be recognized, accepted, and invited out to play. Recognizing and reclaiming the many guises of the Sacred Feminine within help us create a harmonious whole.

Each subpersonality—whether operating at full capacity or distorted through wounding, fear, or dismissal—is organized around a quality that enhances your life. As an example, after Gene and I had been married several years, a new subpersonality came roaring to the fore in me. I named her Brunhilda because she looked like a Viking warrioress with her coned breast plates, horned helmet, and wicked-looking axe. She scared my Terminal Nice Girl subpersonality and irritated the dickens out of Gene, which was, of course, her very necessary job at that time. Brunhilda's quality is strength to stand up for myself. She has softened and matured over the years but can still wield a gentle but resolute axe when needed.

During your day...

✧ Become aware of different subpersonalities as they emerge. These aspects are your friends; delight in them. Some may need a little healing, but each is essential, and the quality they express is beneficial.

✧ Imagine what that quality might be.

Much of spiritual life is self-acceptance, maybe all of it.
—JACK KORNFIELD

GETTING TO KNOW YOU

Getting to know my subpersonalities has been one of the most helpful and healing psychological tools I've ever used. Being aware of the different aspects of myself helps me understand difficult feelings, helps me realize who inside me is experiencing them, and gives me the chance to find out what they want and need in order to feel better. The more I connect with my subpersonalities, the easier it is for me to move into the "I" aspect of my being and become an objective and kind mother/ mentor figure to a hurting sub.

Yesterday was a good example. Due to computer difficulties that included ignorance on my part, my longtime subpersonality Miz Perfection was frustrated to the hilt and as irritable as a PMSing mother of toddler triplets. Gene was trying to be helpful, but all I wanted to do was scream at him to be quiet. Luckily, I thought to ask Miz Perfection what she wanted and needed from me right then. In a smart-aleck tone, she retorted, "I *want* you to knock his block off, but I *need* you to speak calmly and get out." I laughed silently, did as I was told, and avoided hurt feelings. The laughter lightened my mood, and leaving kept me from splashing icky irritation energy on Gene. A win-win.... Feminine wisdom always desires win-win outcomes.

Your subpersonalities can appear as male or female humans, animals, or symbols. In a visualization I did with my son, he discovered a squirrel subpersonality. At that time, no one I knew had an animal, but with Brett's bushy red hair, active personality, and athletic ability, a squirrel was perfect. More importantly, he related to the image. Whoever or whatever appears to you and feels *right* is okay.

Orchestral musicians who understand their own and their colleague's music play easily together. The same is true of you; the more you know, understand, and accept your various subpersonalities, the more harmoniously they can coexist. Internal awareness ups your happiness quotient enormously.

During your day...

❖ If you are a visual person, picture your subpersonalities. If visualization is hard for you, simply get a sense of what they might look like. Name them and begin to explore what makes them tick.

❖ If you are aware of subpersonalities in distress, ask them what they want and need from you right now. Wants can be different from needs.

❖ Have fun. You are getting to know a valuable inner circle of advocates and friends.

The more you know and accept all your selves, the stronger you become.

EMULATING WATER

Water is indispensable and adaptive and, therefore, an apt metaphor for feminine energy. If you've ever seen a flooding river crest or been close to the sea during a ferocious storm, you know firsthand the impressive power and frightening strength of water in agitated action. On the other end of the spectrum, the Grand Canyon is a testament to the patient, long-term power of water.

Yes, water can be dammed and contained, but when gathered together in great enough quantities, it can overcome most obstacles. Now is a great time for the water sprite in all of us to return to Source, break free, and reconstitute ourselves by emulating the fluid, yet determined, feminine aspects of water. Our physical bodies are already approximately 60 percent water; let's saturate our mental, emotional, and spiritual bodies with watery Sacred Feminine energy and invite our complete self to be in the flow.

One great example of peaceful, persistent feminine power is shown in the documentary *Pray the Devil Back to Hell.* It tells of a peace movement called Women of Liberia Mass Action for Peace. Organized by a Liberian social worker, Leymah Gbowee, Muslim and Christian women came together dressed in white to pray for peace and participate in nonviolent protests to demand a resolution to the country's civil war. Their movement eventually led to the election of the first female president of an African nation.

During your day…

✧ As you use and enjoy water, appreciate it's life-
   giving presence.

✧ If you feel constricted or trapped by a situation, imagine
   how water might find her way out or through.

✧ Notice which of your subpersonalities are best able to
   go with the flow.

> *Water is of all things most yielding and can*
> *overwhelm that which is most hard.*
>
> —TAOIST ADAGE

INTEGRATING HEART AND HEAD

In our quest to live balanced, happy lives, learning to integrate the
feminine heart and masculine head energies within our own psyches is
essential. Both energies are God given, and each has beneficial qualities.
Many men and women have recognized that true balance comes from
liberating the feminine in men and the masculine in women. In reality,
almost everything worth doing or being requires both heart and head
attributes to be successful. Life is much easier and more fun when both
are balanced and cooperative.

I've noticed many of us, male and female alike, are expressing more head than heart energy. That's okay as long as your behavior feels comfortable and genuine. Although I can be competitive in games, I don't feel right expressing hard-edged, aggressive energy except in the privacy of my own mind or with a trusted friend who is not the target. In order not to suffer guilt and remorse, I need to transform conquering and controlling mental energy before I talk with someone about issues and misunderstandings. Only after taking the aggression out of my feelings can I engage in a heart-centered discussion with the hope of finding more understanding and a win-win solution for everyone. Others I know find fiery encounters stimulating and fun. No matter what your individual comfort zones, the important thing is to relate to yourself and others authentically.

If you spend a great deal of time in an environment that demands a lot of mind/striving/outer head energy, you instinctively know when it's time to give intuitive/relational/feminine heart energy some attention. On the other hand, if you spend most of your time nurturing your family or in a career such as nursing, your mental head side could probably use some time in the spotlight. Balancing both energies promotes peace of mind, heart, and body.

During your day…

- ✧ With an open mind and heart, notice how much time you spend in your head versus your heart.
- ✧ Does the balance feel like an authentic representation of who you are? If so, great. If not, what changes might be helpful?

> *The authentic self is the soul made visible.*
> —SARAH BAN BREATHNACH

MIRRORING JESUS AND ROSA PARKS

> *Male and female represent the two sides of the great radical dualism. But, in fact, they are perpetually passing into one another. Fluid hardens to solid, solid rushes to fluid. There is no wholly masculine man, no purely feminine woman.*
>
> —MARGARET FULLER

The preceding quote points out the intermingling of energies that Jesus and Rosa Parks so beautifully illustrated in their lives.

As portrayed throughout history, Jesus appears to have been a sterling example of a man who lived from his heart even though residing in a patriarchal era and raised in a male-dominated religion. He reportedly liked and respected women, helped all those who needed it, taught and modeled love and acceptance for all, and forgave under the most extreme circumstances. I imagine him as friendly and outgoing while also requiring silence and solitude to refresh his soul. And he must have been tremendously charismatic and purposeful to impart teachings that still influence millions today. To me, he is the perfect example of unconditional love.

I'm so thankful to my Sunday School teachers who portrayed Jesus as someone to trust rather than fear, and as a result, I've been enamored of him since I was a little girl. To this day, I often feel his presence especially when in need of comforting. To me, Jesus epitomizes integration of heart and head and masculine and feminine energy.

In a very different way, Rosa Parks is also a great example of integration (accidental pun). Although she was actually the second African American woman who refused to give up her seat to a white passenger, her peaceful yet resolute refusal and arrest led to the 1955 Montgomery bus boycott. As a result of the thirteen-month boycott, important changes were made in the existing laws, and Rosa Parks's part in that caused the U.S. Congress to call her the first lady of civil rights and the mother of the freedom movement.

Even if the examples of Jesus and Rosa Parks don't resonate with you, I imagine there are people in your life who have the wonderful ability to combine heart and head energy in complementary ways. Maybe one of those is *you*.

During your day...

- ✧ Be aware of opportunities to use both your heart and head in dealing with simple occurrences.
- ✧ Think of people you know who blend masculine and feminine energies wisely and effectively.
- ✧ Congratulate yourself when your heart and head are in sync.

Allow your life to reflect all aspects of your being.

BEING AMUSED AND EDUCATED BY SHADOW

One of the most fruitful connections we can make is with the shadow aspects of our personalities, for they often represent unhealthy roles we've fallen into or strengths we are not fully expressing. A great way to become acquainted with active shadow sides is through subpersonality exploration. I've already introduced you to two of my shadow aspects, Brunhilda and Miz Perfection. Brunhilda, whose quality is the strength to stand up for myself, is the shadow side of Strong Adult Sue. I needed Brunhilda to show up in her dramatic warrioress form to grab my attention and help me balance her counterpart, Terminal Nice Girl. Miz Perfection is the shadow version of Madame Reliable-Responsible, and not surprisingly, her qualities are reliability and responsibility. In shadow form, however, those beneficial qualities become compulsion and perfectionism. Anxiety, nervousness, and stress alert me to Miz Perfection's presence. Knowing she's in the driver's seat allows me to take over the steering wheel and make more self-supportive choices.

When we are connected to the magical essence of feminine energy, we feel spaciousness, generosity, joy, love, and all the other good stuff. Contrarily, when immersed in our shadow selves, we feel constricted, miserly, depressed, manipulative, victimized, ashamed, bitchy, and sometimes downright mean.

Getting to know and appreciate our shadow sides is enlightening and life-enhancing; however, acting directly from them can be iffy and possibly destructive.

We all have shadow sides. They are invaluable teachers, natural and educational parts of being a multifaceted human being. They can also bring a lot of fun, spice, and excitement to our lives. Given their helpful nature, it is appropriate to greet shadow aspects with open hearts, amusement, and gratitude for the valuable insights they offer about our attitudes, behaviors, and beliefs.

During your day...

> ✧ Tune into what you consider a shadow aspect of yourself. Someone you might call a bitch, whiner, drama queen, or possibly something others have

labeled you. If you can be amused as you get to know this aspect, that's great.

✧ Delve a little deeper and find out if this shadow aspect has insights about you or a current situation or concern. Ask how she can help you.

✧ What about her appeals to you?

Welcomed into our awareness, shadow aspects can be a wellspring of wisdom and entertainment.

LOVIN' LARGE

Recently I was waiting in an overcrowded airport boarding area that served three different gates and offered almost no amenities. People were sitting on the floor, one overstimulated dog was wide-eyed and wiggly, little kids were cranky   as were a few of us bigger kids. Squashed into a cramped two-chair space, with colorful bags and sacks scattered all around them, was a foursome of women having the time of their lives. Their frivolity was contagious, and hearing them laughing and kidding around with each other relieved the uncomfortable tedium of waiting. Unexpectedly, a part of their good-natured bantering gave me an important lesson.

One woman was joking about dieting when her generously proportioned friend retorted, "Honey, I finally decided, since I'm gonna *be* large, I might as well *love* large." I don't know if the double entendre was intended, but the Oprahesque replier seemed A-OK with herself just as she was and appeared to be a person who also loved herself and others in a large way.

When I remember, I adopt her attitude, and instead of likening my own generous body to a Macy's Thanksgiving Day Parade balloon, I affirm *I am built to love large.* It makes a difference, shifts the energy from criticism to love, and that's huge. In a good way.

During your day…

- ✧ Change critical comments about yourself to loving and affirming ones.
- ✧ No matter what your physical size, know that you are made to love large.

A little bit a lovin' makes a whole lotta difference.

2

HAVING COURAGE

Having courage does not mean that we are unafraid.
Having courage and showing courage means we face our
fear. We are able to say, "I have fallen, but I will get up."
—MAYA ANGELOU

The bad news about fear is that it feels terrible and can be paralyzing. The good news is that most fear is learned and, consequently, can be *un*learned. Only the fear of falling and the fear of loud noises are primal and natural. All other fears are learned, including the fear of death.

The powers that be—society, family, church, government— use fear to control us. Employed wisely and sparingly, fear can be a protective learning tool, but all too often, it is wielded as a bludgeon and we are conditioned to be unnaturally fearful. Of course, fear can also be a by-product of traumatic experiences: emotional and physical abuse, rape, abandonment, molestation, dismissal, and neglect, to name only a few. If something traumatic has happened to you, and your fears feel overwhelming, please allow a clergy person, therapist, or other trained professional to help you heal. Sometimes the most courageous thing you can do is accept help.

Although our automatic reactions to fear are fight, flight, and freeze, none of those responses heal and transform fear when used long term. Denying, running from, and ignoring fear allows it to grow unchecked and gives it the power to shroud your essence. The only way to truly *unlearn* and transform fear is to face it, work through it, and act in spite of it. Most women I know have already courageously faced and tamed fear a thousand times over, and I bet you're one of them.

EXAMINING FEAR

Many of us have one or two fears that intermittently raise their heads no matter what our age or situation. One of mine is the fear of not being good enough. As I write this by hand on a yellow legal pad at 4:30 a.m., that familiar face of fear is sitting right here with me. Having awakened from a stress-filled dream about being lost, I can feel my heart pounding and realize tears hover on my lids. A litany of worn-out but well-known phrases churn through my mind. *You shouldn't have... There's not enough time... This won't work... You can't....*

Because it's been a while since I've written a book, I'd forgotten that I always seem to go through whatever I'm writing about. Voilà! Fear is the topic of this chapter, and here I am face to face with the opportunity to examine a familiar one and do something I've never done before by taking you with me on this real-time examination.

Because it usually works well for me, I'm going to explore using the subpersonality querying I wrote about in the first chapter. As I go inward, I notice how my body feels. Not great. Along with the rapid heartbeat, I feel edgy, tired, and sad. *Who is feeling the fear?* The image of a cowering little girl crouched behind a wall comes into my mind. *What's your name?* She quietly responds, *"Failure."* I began to feel compassion for her and long to hug her, but it's too soon for that, so I ask, *"Are you afraid you'll fail at something?"* She nods and, in my mind's eye, I see my four-year-old self staring out the window before dawn watching my mother walk to the bus stop to go to work. With this visual, I realize this fear is an old, old one. As a kid, I always wanted to make my mother happy. More often than not, I felt I failed. Mother didn't ask or expect this from me. For some mysterious soul reason, I took that mission on myself. *"What do you want and/or need from me?"* Crawling out from behind the wall, little Sue responds, *"I just wanted you to see me."* I assure her I do. Tell her I love her. Thank her and tuck her in my heart-pocket.

With this awareness, I now understand that my current fears of failing myself, the publisher, and you if this book isn't up to par or helpful go all the way back to an impossible task I gave myself decades ago. Now I know who within me needs to be reassured and kept safe as "we" write. With this information, I can *see* little Sue.

During your day…

- ✧ If it resonates with you, explore a fear using the sub-personality exercise I did this morning.
- ✧ Courageously and kindly examine fear in our own way.

> *The beautiful thing about fear is,*
> *when you run to it, it runs away.*
> —ROBIN SHARMA

PAYING ATTENTION TO FEAR

Because it elicits painful feelings, fear can easily be seen as the enemy. Actually, fear is like a flashing red light saying, *"Something is not right here; pay attention!"* Intuitively, we understand that message and know fear can be a life-enhancing guide. Even life-*saving* on rare occasions. However, left on its own, fear congeals our life force creating stagnant swamps of unfinished business, unhealed wounds, and regret. Unexplored, fear acts as a huge boot standing on our life force hose.

When you have the courage to pay attention to fear, it can lead you to lightness, healing, increased love, and happiness. Our souls yearn to soar. P'taah, an admired teacher of mine, told his Australian students, "Within all of you there is a spark of Divinity, the Christos, the Source. It is the light filament which connects you with everything and everyone." Unexamined fear dims your divine spark and veils the sweet strands linking you to everything and everyone. On the other hand, paying attention to fear allows it to become an excellent guide to the places within that need healing. Places aching for your attention, love, and understanding. In the light of love, most wounds, worries, and doubts can be healed so that our souls are free to soar for our own enjoyment and the delight of others.

As a caveat, if you don't feel safe exploring fears that present themselves, it's wise to pay attention to that message. Your inner wisdom, the ever-present divine spark, knows what is best for you. Please listen to your qualms and act accordingly. When you're examining fear, it's not unusual to want to be seen and heard during the process. If need be, trusted friends, family members, or professionals can provide a safety net of neutral ears and compassionate hearts as fear guides you toward healing and wholeness.

During your day...

- ✧ Embrace the spark of Divinity within you. Set aside a quiet minute or two to bask in the presence of the Divine.
- ✧ Pay attention to your intuition. She has your back.

Who you are is Divine expression, every facet of you.
Be still and feel. That is all you need to do.
—P'TAAH

WRINGING OUT THE SPONGE

Physics assures us everything is energy, and I've learned by experience that most of us are ultra-absorbent Energy Sponges. A driver flips you off and, wham!, you feel it in your solar plexus, or third chakra. Your teenager manages to be sullen, blaming, and sad in one sentence (if she is speaking at all), and you feel slimed. You are absolutely right; you *have* been slimed. Possibly on purpose from your hormone-laden teen, but we also routinely absorb energy that isn't meant for us, aimed at us, or ours to carry. Energy isn't bound by any delivery system, and negative energy is an equal-opportunity invader. We can look at the news for five minutes and be thoroughly saturated with sadness, disgust, rage, and a million other dense, downer energies. Often we absorb friends' energy or carry a lot more away from Facebook than is healthy for our psyches. Given the amount of energy and information inundating us daily, it's definitely enough to absorb only that which is meant for us.

Sadly, our brains soak up negative energy more readily than they do positive. As Dr. Rick Hanson explains in his book *Buddha's Brain*, "Our brains are Velcro for negative experiences and Teflon for positive ones." Unfortunately, our brains react much as they did in primitive times and tend to compulsively obsess over negatives while sloughing off positive ideas and feelings easily. That fact is high on my list of topics to chat with God about when the time comes.

Luckily, there are ways to protect yourself from unconsciously absorbing others' energy and cleanse yourself when you intuitively know it's needed. A few effective ways to be less spongy are to surround yourself with an impermeable bubble of protection, or imagine being enfolded in beautiful angel wings or, as I've recently been taught, place a protection rose or wall of roses around you to absorb energy that is not yours to manage. Roses are used because, wherever they appear throughout time, symbolize God at work.

Even the best of precautions may not totally protect us sensitive sponges, but there are ways to metaphorically wring them out and flush unwanted energy from our bodies and auras. Years ago, my cherished spiritual mother and teacher, Annabelle, taught me the following discernment technique. If you feel "off" and can't pinpoint what is causing it, prayerfully asking the following questions may help:

- ✧ *If this is my feeling or energy, I ask to understand what it is trying to tell me as soon and deeply as possible.*
- ✧ *If this is not my feeling or energy, I ask that it be gently, but completely, removed from me and returned to its perfect, right person or place.*

Practices such as this one are often more successful when accompanied by mental pictures.

During your day...

- ✧ Protect yourself from rampant slime in whatever ways feel right to you.
- ✧ Give yourself an energy bath if needed.

Have fun wringing yourself free from unwanted excess energy.

OVERESTIMATING STRENGTH

Sometimes our greatest strengths are also our greatest weaknesses. For example, we may let ourselves be treated poorly because we understand the reasons and wounds creating another's behavior. Understanding is a valuable trait of feminine wisdom, but when it leads to accepting the unacceptable, it becomes self-sabotage. When a client, Maddie, tried to understand why her neighbor had stood by while her dog attacked Maddie's, the neighbor—let's call her Cruella—unleashed what professional mediators refer to as a character assassination. Maddie left the conversation reeling but tried to talk with her neighbor again a couple of days later. Cruella continued the assault, almost gleefully attacking everything she knew Maddie valued about herself and her life.

Maddie came to me because she was distraught that someone whom she had considered a friend, and done a lot for, could think of her as such a terrible person.

Although Maddie was heartsick, she understood Cruella's attitude was probably fueled by jealousy and kept attributing Cruella's behavior to wounds from a difficult childhood and abusive marriage. As we talked, it became obvious that Cruella was entrenched and not interested in working things out. While Maddie's understanding of Cruella's motivation was commendable, trying to make her feel differently was probably impossible and even a little grandiose. Because Maddie is a therapist noted for her communication skills, she wanted to believe there was something she could do.

Maddie's strong need to be liked, exacerbated by the fact Cruella had bad-mouthed her in the neighborhood, blinded her to reality and led her to overestimate her power to change the situation. Maddie had the courage to recognize she had less clout than she wanted, and our work turned to helping her heal her wounds and manage her deep need to be seen and liked.

As strong, compassionate, and understanding women, we are sometimes under the illusion we can make *everything* better. Not so. If you find yourself thinking along those lines, it's time to ask whether you are overestimating your influence and, if so, why?

During your day...

- ✧ Accept yourself as is.
- ✧ Have the courage to admit—and be okay with—not having all the answers all the time.

> *What you think of me is none of my business.*
> —TERRY COLE-WHITTAKER

AVOIDING OVERSTIMULATION

Do you suffer from FOMO? Does FOMO keep you on the go even when exhaustion is tugging at your sleeve like a sleep-deprived two-year-old? Does FOMO have you tethered to social media sites or glued to twenty-four-hour news channels until you're drowning in a tsunami of misinformation? If you are scratching your head wondering what FOMO is, you and I may be from the same generation. At Bookless Club, I learned from a younger neighbor that FOMO stands for **F**ear **O**f **M**issing **O**ut. Let's talk about a different FOMO, **F**ear **O**f **M**axing **O**ut.

During crises, most of us are able to muster astonishing strength and stamina. Understandable causes such as illness, new babies, travel, deadlines, financial concerns, and natural disasters stretch us to the limit of our endurance but are a necessary part of life. And most are intermittent. In today's accelerated and densely populated society, however, much overstimulation, or maxed-outness, is relentlessly constant and of our own choosing.

It takes awareness to notice when you're overstimulated and a lot of courage to actually *do* something about it. Turning off devices, muting sound, getting enough sleep, saying no to a request for help or—harder still—an enticing invitation can be very difficult to do, especially if we're addicted to the rush of being in the know. But, for the sake of our poor beleaguered nervous systems, we need to try.

Our technology guru, Michael, told us that shutting down our computers each night protects them from invasion. With a wink, he said, "Computers need to rest, too." So do overtaxed nervous systems. If a nervous system is kept at red alert too long, it may give up and shut itself down. Just the opposite of computers, a shuttered nervous system is *more* susceptible to invasion from interlopers such as illness, brain fog, anxiety, depression, insomnia, and emotional burnout.

If you are deeply fearful of missing out, it won't be easy, but please do yourself and your nervous system a big favor and have the courage to alleviate maxing out in all the ways you can.

During your day…

- ✧ Designate a device-free zone at work or home and spend ten minutes or more there.
- ✧ Use earplugs or headphones to mask energy-draining noise.

✧ Become aware of maxed-out emotional and physical fallout you may be experiencing.

FOMO: **F**or **O**ne **M**oment **O**nly, *give yourself a stimulation break.*

STAYING IN THE MOMENT

Are you adept at spending most of your time in the moment, or do you wander off into what author Hugh Prather referred to as "rehearsing difficulties to come?" Most of us habitually spend our time reflecting on what happened in the past or fretting about what may occur in the future. Interestingly, fear loves to hang out in both the past and the future but is less comfortable in the here and now. Courage, on the other hand, almost always resides in the current moment. We can think about past courageous acts or imagine how we might be courageous in the future, but we *are* courageous moment by moment.

Given that reality, one of the best ways to tame fear is to live in the moment as much as possible. A friend of mine is terribly afraid of speaking in front of people. If she knows she will be making an announcement at church, she is fearful until the task is completed. If she's asked to speak on the spur of the moment, after the initial shock, she does just fine. In the moment, she has the courage and ability. In anticipation, she fears she doesn't have either.

Okay, living in the moment sounds great, but how do we actually *do* it? As with many, many things in life, awareness is the key. We need to be aware of where our thoughts are, which means we need to have the courage to live mindfully. If you become aware your thoughts have strayed into the past or are forging ahead into the future, you can consciously choose to bring your awareness back to this moment, back into the here and now.

We are only truly alive *now*. Yesterday's self is a memory and tomorrow's is a mystery.

During your day...

✧ If you notice yourself feeling edgy or fearful, bring your attention into the here and now. Become aware of your surroundings, the temperature, what you can see, whether your body is sitting or standing. After a minute or two, return your attention to your feelings. Are they the same or maybe a little different?

✧ Set an alarm on your phone for a few different times during the day. When it chimes, mindfully return to the present moment if you're not already there.

A few mindful moments make a world of difference.

3

PRACTICING
SELF-COMPASSION

---

*Love yourself first and everything else falls into line. You really
have to love yourself to get anything done in this world.*

—LUCILLE BALL

One thing I noticed in private practice was that most clients' wants
and needs could be summarized in three short yearnings: *See me. Hear
me. Hold me.* Sadly, there was also an occasional heart-breaking *Protect
me*, especially in abuse and addiction situations. Tapping into the
compassionate wisdom and intuitive power of your internal Sacred
Feminine allows you to excel at seeing, hearing, and holding others.
Your innate feminine energy knows how to recognize people as they
are and long to be seen, recognize unspoken feelings between words,
and offer genuine support and solace.

For most of us, being able to see, hear, and hold others comes
pretty naturally, but offering the same compassionate attentiveness to
ourselves is more elusive. Do you view yourself with understanding

and gentle eyes? Can you listen to your thoughts and words with an honest and compassionate heart? Do you treat yourself in ways that promote balance and harmony in all four aspects of your being: physical, emotional, mental, and spiritual? When hurting, are you able to soothe yourself as an affectionate and tender mother or friend would?

If you answered no to some or all of those questions, please know you are not alone. Many of us were *taught* that self-care and self-compassion were unacceptable and, in some cases, even sinful. The opposite is resoundingly true.

The better you know yourself, the more compassionate you can be with yourself. The more compassionate you are, the more secure and confident you feel. The more secure and self-confident you feel, the more energy you have to care for and about other people. Harsh self-judgment and reproach act as emotional samurai swords slicing gaping holes in your energy field and draining your life force. The richer your life-force account, the more effortlessly you can be present to yourself and others. Overflow-giving is healthier and more satisfying for both giver and receiver.

This chapter explores ways you can know yourself better and, in doing so, become your own compassionate friend and advocate. Since we have a lot to get done to make our personal lives happier and the world a better place, let's take Lucille Ball's advice: love ourselves first, and get crackin'!

UNDERSTANDING YOUR SENSITIVITY QUOTIENT

Years ago, as I was first reading Dr. Elaine Aron's *The Highly Sensitive Person: How to Thrive When the World Overwhelms You*, I would have burst into singing "Getting to Know You" from the *King and I* had I not been on a plane. Instead, I burst into tears.

All my life I'd harbored a secret belief that I was somehow fundamentally flawed. For as long as I could remember, I'd heard or said to myself: *"You're too emotional. You're too persnickety about smells... sounds... crowds... criticism. What's wrong with you? Just ignore it like I do. You're too sensitive!"* And here was a research psychologist, college professor, and psychotherapist, herself a highly sensitive person, or HSP, telling me I was neither crazy nor a bona fide bitch.

These two sentences from Dr. Aron's book were life changing and a profound relief to me: "Having a sensitive nervous system is normal, a basically neutral trait. You probably inherited it." (Ah, so... that explains a lot about my family.) About 15 to 20 percent of the population falls in this category. However, those of you drawn to books like this are more likely to have HSP tendencies than the population as a whole. Characteristics of a highly sensitive nervous system are sensitivity, naturally, and *overarousal* from sensory and energetic stimuli of all kinds. What most people can ignore, HSPs are highly disturbed by, especially stimuli over which they have no control.

Since my dad described my largely sleepless infant self as "an eel with insomnia," I imagine I came in as an HSP and, unless things change dramatically, will go out as one also. But, at least, I now have information that helps me understand myself more completely and, consequently, be a better friend to myself. Knowing about my nervous system sensitivity has helped my husband understand my responses also. Awareness has been good for both of us individually and for our marriage.

During your day…

- ✧ If you suspect you, or someone you care about, may be highly sensitive, you can find Dr. Aron's simple diagnostic test at *hsperson.com/test*.
- ✧ Getting to know you definitely helps getting to like you.

> *Seeing yourself as you truly are is essential for understanding your idiosyncrasies.*

KEEPING YOUR HEART VISIBLE

Much to my surprise, Cynthia burst into tears the minute she sat down. As I quietly waited for her tears to subside, I mused about her, a woman I knew socially but had never seen as a client. To the outside world, Cynthia had it all—a successful career, a nice husband, good kids, and a beautiful house. Yet, she was crying as if her heart were broken. Turns out, it was.

As Cynthia's story unfolded, it became clear that she had not been happy in her marriage for several years but didn't understand why because nothing had changed, and everything was going smoothly. She'd run through all the chastisements we often flog ourselves with: stop feeling sorry for yourself, be grateful for what you have, your life is a cakewalk compared to so and so's. Berating herself heaped shame on top of unhappiness. A revealing self-guided meditation had led her to therapy.

In her visualization, Cynthia was comfortably seated in her home. She invited her inner wisdom to show her what was causing her discontent. One of her daughters appeared, and Cynthia noticed that her own heart began to ache and she saw it was bruised and battered. Not surprised, because she and her daughter had recently had a hurtful confrontation, she was able to heal her heart and forgive them both for their falling out. Another daughter, with whom she was close now after a painful past, came into her mind's eye, and Cynthia's heart began to bleed. This, too, was easily healed and forgiven. With her healed heart still visible, Cynthia sensed her husband approaching. When he appeared, her heart completely evaporated in a puff of gray smoke. In her head she heard, *"My heart is invisible to him."* Much to her sorrow, she then heard, *"And you've let it become invisible to you, also."*

It turned out that, though a wonderful man, Cynthia's husband was emotionally unavailable. An eternal optimist, she had held out hope he would change. The imagery helped her accept the fact that he probably would never be able to provide the emotional support for which she longed. After deeply grieving the loss of that dream, Cynthia decided she wanted to accept her husband as he was and enjoy what the relationship did offer—which was a lot, she assured me. A very strong woman, Cynthia vowed to take loving care of herself and carefully honor her own wants and needs. The other day, for the first time in several years, I saw her, and she is very happy. She has created a rich life surrounded by loving and available friends, has come to cherish her marriage as is, and compassionately cares for her heart daily.

During your day...

- ✧ If your heart is anything less than content, spend some quiet time tuning in to what it is feeling and what it might want or need from you.
- ✧ Keep an eye on your heart.

> *The heart knows the way. Run in that direction.*
> —RUMI

DRINKING FROM THE WELL

One of the most magical attributes you have is your imagination. And one of the most compassionate things you can do for yourself is to inspire, uplift, and soothe your spirit with it. Let's play with imagination now. If you are not a visual person, that's okay; just allow yourself to *sense* the experience. However your unique imagination works is great. Close your eyes, if you're in a safe place to do so, and imagine yourself sitting beside a well in a friendly and beautiful natural setting. If what you see or sense doesn't appeal to you, without any effort, allow that scene to fade and invite another to take its place. There's nothing to do but enjoy where you are and what you feel. Immerse yourself in the experience. Notice the sounds, the sights, and the essence of this gift from your imagination.

If you have a question, ask it and retrieve the answer from the well in whatever way occurs to you.

While I believe with all my heart that everything I want and need can be found within the wellspring of my own being, my mind often disagrees and, under its influence, I forget. Forgetting your internal well is easy, especially when you feel beleaguered, scared, ill, out of your depth with crises, or just plain exhausted. But, if you can remember— and find the time and quiet—to go to your inner well, it's usually refreshing and rejuvenating. I never know what my well will look like when I remember to retreat to it. Today's was under the sea—a first for me—and several dolphins were playing nearby. After asking my question, I didn't have time to get the answer from the well because a dolphin immediately popped up with a sign in her mouth that said, "YES!" I laughed because my rational mind had wondered how the hell I was going to get anything out of a well already submerged in water.

Visiting your well gives you the opportunity to be seen, heard, and held by your compassion-filled Higher Self.

During your day…

✦ There is within you an overflowing well filled with the sweet nectar of Spirit. Treat yourself to a visit.

> *We are moving into a new paradigm, leaving the old structures behind. Where do we go for our guidance? I suggest to you that we have no place but our own well. We all have this well inside.*
> —MARION WOODMAN

ALTERING MISPERCEPTIONS

Interestingly, our strength and ability to love are both more dependable when augmented by self-compassion, yet many of us still carry the misperception that loving ourselves is selfish. My phone dictionary defines selfish as "devoted to or caring only for oneself; concerned primarily with one's own interests, benefits, welfare, etc., regardless of others." Is that you? Nope, me neither.

You and I both understand that self-care and self-compassion are wise and healthy choices, but I bet you sometimes fear you're being selfish if you put yourself first. I know I do. But, thankfully, only rarely now that I've ripened into crone category. And, of course, at this age my responsibilities are a fraction of what they were when all four kids were home and both Gene and I were working. Sometimes we look at each other and say, "How did we *do* that?" One reason was we had each other, and I'm sure many of you reading do not have that luxury. However, memories of a four-year stint as a single mom with little money are branded on my psyche, so I know it's incredibly challenging.

It's time to give yourself a break and alter any misperceptions you may be harboring regarding self-compassion and self-care. Self-compassion and self-care are necessary, essential, crucial, vital.... They restore your energy, ground your strength, rest your weary body and mind, and refill the vessel of your being from which I'm sure you are more often serving others rather than yourself.

During your day…

✧ Give self-compassion a shot. If you question whether an action or lack of action is selfish, imagine what you would tell a dear friend if she asked you about a similar decision.
✧ Nourish best from overflow.

> *Self-care means giving the world the best of you instead of what is left of you.*
> —KATIE REED

BEING HERE, NOW

One of the best ways to practice self-compassion is being aware of where you spend most of your waking hours. Is it in the present moment, the unknown future, or the pitfalls of the past?

Of course, it's great to revisit the fun stuff down Memory Lane as well as experience an exhilarating spine-tingle or two peeking up Anticipation Alley. But it is self-compassionate to be wary of the maybe-never-gonna-happen worries dotting the landscape along Fear Freeway into the future and cautious of the depressions and rough patches marring the surface of Regret Road leading to the past.

Whether we do or don't have past regrets or future fears, it's healthier for all of us to spend the majority of our time in the present rather than the past or the future. I know this is probably the million and oneth time you've heard it's wise to stay in the present moment and that my metaphor is incredibly corny, but maybe it's silly enough to stick. For both of us. I often used to take the rough road back into the past and wallow around in regrets and resentments I couldn't change, but I don't do it much anymore. I imagine that the many years and much practice I've had learning how to heal the past, release resentments, and make amends have made the difference. I don't spend much time thinking about the future either. Maybe that's one of the perks of aging, or possibly, I finally know and love myself enough to believe I can handle whatever *does* come along, so why worry? This is a huge relief, as I used to be a wizard at worrying.

That said, if things in your past *can* be healed or amends need to be made, by all means, do it. If deep-seated wounds are still waiting for healing, please approach them gently and with help, if need be. Just today, I was feeling grateful to recently have had help in cleaning out a festering old wound and being able to forgive myself for allowing it and the other for inflicting it. If you know you need to make amends, give yourself the gift of at least attempting to bring the situation into balance and harmony. If that is impossible in the real world because the person is dead, unavailable, or unapproachable, you can still complete the process in the spiritual realm. This, too, may require some guidance.

During your day...

- ✧ Consciously bring yourself into the present moment four or five times.
- ✧ If past wounds, given or received, need healing, take one small step toward doing so.
- ✧ While in the present moment, say "Hi" to your soul.

> *Human **beings** can only **be** in the present.*
> *In the past, we **were**. In the future, we **will be**.*

ASKING WHAT'S GOOD FOR YOU

> *Unlike self-criticism, which asks if you're good enough,*
> *self-compassion asks, what's good for you?*
> —KRISTIN NEFF

I'm having a serious nap-attack. If I were to ask what's good for me right now, what would the answer be? *Lie down, Dearie.* As an experiment, and because I was *really* tired, I followed the advice and stretched out on the guest bed for a thirty-minute rest with my little dog, Lily, tucked against my side. Although I'd love to say we drifted off into a sweet slumber filled with even sweeter dreams, that didn't happen. Real life happened, as it often does. To start with, Lily was shivering. For an almost-ten-pound dog, her shivers are surprisingly intense, more like Lilliputian earthquakes. When she finally got warm enough to stop trembling, my husband came creeping in—I had forgotten he wanted to take her on a late afternoon walk—and took her off the bed. Fifteen minutes had elapsed. It took him another five minutes to get them both ready to go. (All this was happening right outside the room where I was "resting.") As you can imagine, I did not peacefully nod off in the remaining ten minutes. After the annoyance passed, I chuckled, guessing you'd probably be able to relate to my aborted foray into asking what was good for me.

Even so, asking what's good for you is a wonderfully self-compassionate habit to adopt. However, depending on how many responsibilities and obligations you shoulder, it may also be one you need to be very, very committed to in order not to become discouraged when what's good for you doesn't sit well with what others think is good for them. While we often chuckle and nod our heads in rueful agreement when seeing the adage "If momma ain't happy, ain't nobody happy" on a T-shirt or plaque, truthfully, in most families momma is the happy-maker. How can an *un*happy-maker help anyone else be happy? Simply, the energy of an unhappy momma is enough to dampen the atmosphere in most homes.

Therefore, prioritizing what is good for you is doing a favor to everyone with whom you relate, live, work, and play. But that favor will come to fruition only when you follow through and let yourself *do* what is good for you.

Set yourself up for success by being realistic in your answers to the question "What is good for me?"

During your day…

✧ To get in the habit, two or three times a day, ask yourself, "What is good for me right now?"

✧ If possible, do it. If not possible now, do it ASAP.

> *You can only **do** what's good for you*
> *when you **know** what's good for you.*

SHARING EMOTIONS WISELY

Self-compassion is one of our highest callings, and emotion one of our most valuable gifts. Why, then, do the two often collide? Ignorance and fear, most likely. In the grand scheme of our development, only recently has the mental health community encouraged gently facing feelings or viewed self-compassion as an attribute rather than a selfish indulgence. We are still in the process of integrating the "new" information into the deep recesses of our well-trained, ignore-feelings/think-of-self-last brains.

The intensity of emotion also scares us. We ignore and repress emotion for fear it will overwhelm and defeat us. One of my most important tasks as a hospice worker was to help people face their powerful feelings of grief and, sometimes, regret and be there for them when they did. Even Loretta, who collapsed into an emotional abyss for two weeks, told me later that her time "in the pit" was good, a crash course in empathy and understanding. The outpouring of love and nurturing she received during her experience facilitated her healing. Friends housed, fed, and kept her safe. Once or twice they brought her to my office, where she sat wrapped in a blanket quietly sobbing or just *being*. I hadn't known her before grief knocked her down, but I respected her friends' assessment of her innate strength and their belief she'd be okay. As a hospice worker herself, she now passes on the love she experienced and the empathy she learned.

With good reason, we also fear what will happen if we share our deepest feelings with those we love. In a few cases, our concerns are wise. Some people are *not* able to deal with raw, honest emotion and may run away when faced with yours. While that can definitely feel like a personal rejection, it's really about *them*, not you. If you have explained what you need from them while sharing and they still downplay your feelings, tune out, try to fix you, shame you, or suggest ten thousand ways to "get over it," therapy might help. But, for now, they are not safe people with whom to share intensely painful feelings. Not because they don't love you or care about your feelings, but because their *own* feelings are triggered by yours, and they can't handle it. For your own well-being, lovingly choose to share only the lighter stuff with them.

Because burying emotion often wreaks physical, mental, and emotional havoc—road rage, for example—it is vital and self-loving to share, but *only* in safe places and with safe people. Sharing intense and vulnerable emotions with trusted people allows you to mine the wisdom and insight to be found within them.

During your day…

- ✧ Know with whom you can safely share tender, excruciating emotions.
- ✧ For both your sakes, forgive and understand those with whom you cannot.

Emotion can introduce you to vast reservoirs of inner wisdom.

KNOWING YOU ARE GOOD ENOUGH IS NO LONGER GOOD ENOUGH

An annoying title, I know. I laughed out loud when it came to me in the shower. And knowing you're good enough in some things—shucking corn, writing code, singing the "Star Spangled Banner"—is still okay but, overall, we really do need to accept our own excellence and revel in our superpowers because we *all* have them! Sometimes they are huge, long-term, and life-or-death important. What springs to mind is our daughter surviving surgery, chemotherapy, and radiation while raising three well-adjusted boys and, when well again, using her experience to make the world a safer place. That took a truckload of superpowers. On the other hand, some days, simply making it through the next minute is a superpower. Depending on circumstances, making the best decision can be a superpower. Taking care of a sick child calls for stamina and strength we couldn't imagine. Telling the truth in a tough situation. Stretching a few dollars to cover many necessities requires canniness, creativity, and cojones. All superpowers.

Let's apply Rudyard Kipling's philosophy "I always prefer to believe the best of everybody; it saves so much trouble" to ourselves. Believing the best of yourself is, in itself, a superpower. The compassion and kindness inherent in self-belief empower you to *become* whatever is needed in any given moment. I know it can sometimes be hard to believe the best of yourself. Once, in a dream, Jesus and Mary both looked lovingly at me and said, "Sue, you are *good*." Even with such high-powered reassurance, do I always believe the best of myself? Well, no, but *almost* always now. With years of practice and lots of help from superpower-endowed others, I am a zillion times better at knowing I'm doing the best I can, seeing my heart as truly good, and even being able to say, "Damn, Sue, that was *good*!" on occasion. Please know if I—once the self-trashing queen—can do it, you can also. Seeing the best in ourselves saves a *lot* of trouble.

During your day…

⬥ Notice three actions, attitudes, or attributes about yourself that could be seen as superpowers. Have fun with it.

⬥ Create a superheroine persona for yourself or adopt one already out there. Again, please have fun with it.

⬥ Believe the best of two people… one of them being you.

Being me is my superpower.
—Anonymous (usually a woman)

FINDING AMUSEMENT

What a great friend we would be if we could lighten our friends' burdens and shine light into every dark corner of their lives. Most of us probably already do a lot of that, as we are natural light-bearers and love dispelling gloom and darkness wherever and whenever we can. As I said before, being able to see, hear, and hold others helps dissipate the darkness of loneliness and despair, and humor is a great leavening agent for almost all situations. Hopefully, we also compassionately sprinkle darkness-obliterating fairy dust upon ourselves as well.

Above and beyond that, wouldn't it be wonderful if we could lighten our lives by finding amusement in many experiences much of the time? I learned this idea from one of my favorite spiritual teachers, Mary Bell Nyman, who believes that the ability to find amusement in ourselves and our circumstances is one of the most life-enhancing habits we can acquire. Being a lover of laughter and chuckles, I wholeheartedly agree with Mary Bell and decided to adopt an Attitude of Amusement as much as possible. I was doing really well in my amusement practice until...

One of the realities of life is there will probably always be an "until" and mine was the advent of surprise construction in back of our house. We knew there would eventually be construction across the creek and that the zoning was light industrial. What we didn't know was that light industrial includes warehouses. This warehouse is a behemoth; the side toward our house will be 45 feet tall and 165 feet wide. The developers are building a berm—which we've dubbed Mt. Baldy—to block out half the height, but the size of the berm itself has already changed the entire feel of our home, our sanctuary. Plus, since noise is my nemesis, the construction itself is crazy-making. I'm sure if the same earth movers were creating a park, the noise might not seem like such an affront. An Intention toward Amusement helps a tiny little bit.

Although I am nowhere near finding amusement in this particular situation, I am beginning to hold an Attitude of Amusement about many other things, and doing so is lightening and leavening my life in wonderful ways.

During your day...

* ⋄ Set your sights on amusement.
* ⋄ Notice little things that make you smile and lighten your heart, if only a smidgeon. (Kitty videos are A-OK.)
* ⋄ Lighten your attitude toward one of your own foibles, if possible.

> *God, grant me the serenity to accept the things*
> *I cannot change; courage to change the things I*
> *can; and wisdom to know the difference.*
>
> *And an Attitude of Amusement especially*
> *when serenity, courage, and wisdom elude me.*
>
> —REINHOLD NIEBUHR (AND ME)

SHOWERING UNCONDITIONAL COMPASSION

Showering is such a tender feminine concept. Soft April showers bring May flowers, bridal showers, welcoming baby showers; showering kids with love and praise, showering gratitude on those who gift us, and showering blessings as a natural part of our daily modus operandi. If you aren't already doing so, now is the moment to begin showering unconditional compassion upon the person in your skin—you!

As a general rule, women tend to have *conditional* compassion for themselves. *If* I meet this standard, *if* I'm always nice, *when* I lose 120 pounds, *when* I get a better job, *as soon as* the kids are okay. Unfortunately, if conditions are too harsh, or rely on someone else's happiness, we'll never be able to attain them. Therefore, showering *unconditional* compassion upon all aspects of ourselves is the only way to go.

We may also be choosy about who within us is worthy of compassion. For instance, I'm able to be gentle and kind to myself when I'm sad, but it's much harder for me to shower my overstimulated, electrified-nervous-system Bitch subpersonality with anything but impatience. Her name is a giveaway, isn't it?

To prime the pump, bring to mind someone or something you often shower with unconditional love and compassion. It can be anyone or anything—a partner, a child, or a pet. If you're a gardener, you may choose flowers. Picture the recipient of your compassion and notice what it feels like to shower them/it with unconditional positive regard. Gently breathe in the feeling. Become more deeply aware of how it feels to be a conduit of unconditional compassion. With no effort, allow that picture to fade and very tenderly imagine an image of you taking its place. Keep breathing and continue to feel compassion flowing gently toward you from you. If the flow has faltered, say something encouraging like "It's okay" or "I wish only good for you" and allow the gentle flow to resume. In whatever way comes to you, shower this aspect of yourself with blessings.

If showering yourself with unconditional compassion is a struggle, please be kind to yourself and take the small-step approach. Go back to the experience of sending compassion to someone or something other than yourself. For your soul to become comfortable with self-compassion, take as long as you need sending it out to another. Eventually, when it feels doable, allow compassion to shower an image of you.

Tiny drops of intentional other-directed compassion can grow into a gentle shower of self-compassion.

During your day...

⋄ Entertain the idea of unconditional compassion by becoming aware of the conditions you impose on self-love and self-care. Jotting them down can be helpful.

⋄ Eliminate one condition a day, or one a week, for as long as it takes.

Do unto self as you do unto others.

4

GROWING IN THE KILN
OF RELATIONSHIP

*One of the oldest human needs is having
someone wonder where you are when
you don't come home at night.*

—MARGARET MEAD

Feminine energy, wisdom, and power are relational. We thrive on
connection and companionship. When our relationships with ourselves
and others are going smoothly, we feel centered and grounded, able
to take on the world. However, when a relationship is askew, we feel
out of balance, bereft, and anxious to make it right. Relationships are
our ballast and barometer; they warm our hearts; and, yes, sometimes
they curdle our blood. Relationships are also the best personal growth
workshops we could ever attend. Out of their bountiful lessons grew the
acronym FGOs. The *G* and *O* stand for growth opportunities; please
use any *F* word you like to complete the thought. Because we need
relationships and can be so vulnerable within them, they are hot beds of

transformation. No matter the nature of a relationship—parent, child, spouse, friend, sibling, frenemy, neighbor, colleague—many become mirrors reflecting our wonderfulness, weirdness, and weakness. Both our shortcomings and saintliness are reflected in our relationships. This can make them both exhilarating and exhausting. For most women, the term *casual relationship*, for any with a smidgen of personal depth, is an oxymoron.

Of course, your major relationship is with yourself, and your strength is stabilized when founded on self-love and respect. But, because we concentrate on self-awareness, self-love, and self-compassion throughout the entire book, this chapter focuses mostly on your relationships with others.

GIVING UNCONDITIONAL KINDNESS

Kindness is not optional if we are to honor and embody feminine energy and, by doing so, help bring balance and harmony to our seriously lop-sided world. Kindness is especially important in relationships because, in them, imperfections, illusions, delusions, and denials are burned away, and we are purified and made stronger. I refer to relationship as a kiln because, like pottery, which is made beautiful and serviceable in the intense heat of a kiln, the same is true for us within the intensity of relationship. Since we're all in the relationship fire together, wouldn't it be smart to invite kindness to join us? No matter how satisfying or unsatisfying any relationship is in the present moment, at the very least, kindness can elevate the energy. Kindness is possible in most situations and using it sets an intention toward love and growth.

In Theravada Buddhism, metta—which translates to loving-kindness—is a meditation focused on the development of unconditional love for all beings. While we may not achieve unconditional love for all beings, with intention and a little effort, we can get close to it in our relationships. To me, loving-kindness (or metta, if you prefer) doesn't feel warm and fuzzy all the time; sometimes it is merely wishing myself or another person well. A simple metta prayer for myself might be *"May I be peaceful. May I be well. May I feel loved and loving."* If I were about to engage in a possibly difficult talk with my husband, my prayer might be *"May I be able to listen well. May I come to understanding. May I be kind."* In the same situation, my metta prayer, or wish, for him could be *"May you be peaceful. May you be calm. May you come to understanding."* Before learning about metta, my pre-serious-talk "prayers" were more along the lines of *"May you see how wrong you are"* or *"Hopefully, you'll actually listen!"* Surprisingly enough, serious talks seem to go better than they used to....

Kindness softens hard edges, adds value, and imparts positive juju to most circumstances.

During your day...

- ✧ Give yourself a little loving-kindness by putting your own well wishes into the following phrase: "May I be_____. May I_____. May I_____."
- ✧ Choose one loved one for whom to do a loving-kindness prayer.
- ✧ Choose one less-than-loved-one for whom to do the same.
- ✧ Do one small act of kindness for yourself and one for someone else.

Be kind whenever possible.
It is always possible.
—Dalai Lama

DROPPING THE MOTHER LODE

Motherhood ricochets us between extremes. Being a mother and talking honestly with many other mothers, I've come to believe that mothering is the most intensely emotional relationship there is. Nothing is more exhilarating or exhausting. The joy of watching our babies—whether grown under our hearts or adopted from them—sleeping and making sweet sounds is almost unbearably joyous. On the other end of the spectrum, nothing compares to the searing pain experienced when our children are in distress. Whether they are ill, injured, dying, or suffering consequences from their own or others' bad choices, we walk through fire. If they don't like us or treat us badly, we are catapulted into the deepest abyss.

And guilt... guilt is the perpetual Mother Lode. A card I saw proclaimed "Behind every great kid is a mom who's pretty sure she's screwing it up." I don't know about you, but that pretty much sums it up for me. I especially felt guilty about what I considered my inadequate mothering of my first child. The adage "The moment a child is born, a mother is born also" helped assuage some of my guilt, but like many of us, I took a long time to forgive myself enough to be free from the mother-guilt burden. Truthfully, forgiving ourselves is the only answer. In reality, 99.7 percent of us do the best we can and deserve forgiveness for whatever we did, or didn't do, that we regret.

While the vast majority of us are not negligent or abusive mothers to others, we can be to ourselves. This is too bad because our kids grow up and need mothering only occasionally, if at all, while we can benefit from an internal Good Mother for our entire lives. I originally mistyped that as *God Mother*, rather than *Good Mother*, and actually think that's an appropriate analogy. How great it would be to have a goddess-like energy within that we could count on at all times. I'm going to follow my own possibly divinely orchestrated typo and internalize a God Mother, and invite you to do the same.

During your day...

- ✧ Gently, but honestly, ask yourself if there are beneficial mothering changes you could implement. If there are and you don't know how to make them happen, it is wise and loving to all concerned to seek help.
- ✧ Through forgiveness, drop whatever mother lode you are carrying. I am sure you do/did the best you can/could.
- ✧ Be a good mother—a God Mother—to yourself. Speak and act in nurturing and supportive ways to yourself. Be the angel on your own shoulder.

> *There's no way to be a perfect mother and*
> *a million ways to be a good one.*
>
> —JILL CHURCHILL

COMMUNICATING FROM THE HEART

Communication is the maypole around which the colorful ribbons of relationship revolve. When communication is clear, clean, and heartfelt, relationships thrive. If communication is convoluted, critical, or dishonest, relationships wither. Communication creates connection.

Via communication, we share feelings, come to understandings, glean information, and order from Amazon. Communication is the glue that holds relationships together. Ironically, it's also the major sticking point in many close relationships.

One of the reasons communication gets gummed up in close relationships is that the dearer someone is to us, the more vulnerable we are. A misunderstanding with your spouse, child, or treasured friend affects you quite differently than a miscommunication with an acquaintance does. In closer relationships, your feelings run deeper, and consequently, it's more important to feel heard and understood. Because a high level of vulnerability leads to a higher probability of hurt or disappointment—both *to* you and *from* you—it's best to postpone serious communication until your feelings are less volatile.

One of the signs of maturity is the ability to postpone gratification, and nowhere is it more important to practice than in the art of communication. That's been a hard lesson for me to learn because, if things have gone awry, I want to make them better *now*. But, because it's so easy to place blame and shame on one another when our own wounds are fresh and bleeding, premature communication usually creates more separation than understanding.

As I've staggered toward mature, heart-full communication, it's been helpful to adhere to two goals when engaging in serious discussions:

⟡ **Better understanding**: How and why did we get
to the point of needing this conversation? How do you

feel? What do you need? Here is how I got here, how I feel, and what I need.

✧ **Increased closeness**: By understanding each other more completely, and wanting both of us to have what we want and need, we can feel less vulnerable and more connected.

I've also learned that I cannot communicate honestly and without an edge until I've soothed my wounds with the balm of my own acceptance and love. Only then can I let go of righteous expectations of the other person. This is not easily done sometimes and often takes more time than I wish it did.

To communicate from my heart, I must first let go of angst and expectations.

During your day…

✧ When communicating, it's good to remember we are all vulnerable.

✧ Gently tend to your wounds before trying to "make it all better" with the person who hurt you. Sometimes making it better is not possible.

Communication is to relationships what breath is to life.
—Virginia Satir

ACCEPTING FAMILY FOIBLES
(AND PROTECTING YOURSELF!)

I know from my own life, and as a former therapist, that family foibles and failures can be excruciatingly painful. For many of us, it takes great strength to heal from childhood wounds.

Humor helps.

I asked my friend Anita how her Thanksgiving with family had been. Throwing back her head and laughing, she replied, "My family puts the *fun* in dysfunctional." She told a few stories about the holiday, laughing as she spoke. Hearing one experience that would have crushed me, I asked, "How can you laugh about something like that?" She told me she had gone to therapy about her childhood "stuff" and decided during one session that her family was weird, regularly mean, but they were here to stay, so around them she would "be a duck." Anita explained that being a duck helps protect her from absorbing their meanness as she imagines their put-downs rolling off her back. Grinning, she said, "Just so's ya know, I have to go outside and quack sometimes to remind myself!" Wisely, Anita shared the duck-defense with her sister, and they slip outside together when needed. It's good to have a humor-buddy when possible.

I'm reminded of a story I've shared before about my experience at the gorilla enclosure in San Diego's zoo. A large gorilla appeared angry. He paced back and forth, growled at his enclosure mates, stared menacingly at us voyeuristic viewers, and eventually threw feces at us as he howled. We all ducked, but it was a little scary. As we were backing away, I said, "Oh my gosh! That was just like being around Gladys!" (my sister who is no longer alive—not her real name). From then on, to gear myself up for visits that included Gladys, I'd remind myself I was going to the gorilla enclosure and better be prepared to duck. Having a humor connection helped me take the situation—which I had tried to change for decades and failed—more lightly. To keep myself safe, I also erected an energetic feces-free zone around me.

During your day...

✧ Acknowledge that healing lingering childhood wounds is not easy but is essential. You have the strength and wisdom to love yourself to happiness.

✧ Accept the fact you may not be on the same page as family members, but you are in the same library.

✧ Know there's usually something "fun" to learn from families.

> *A dysfunctional family is any family*
> *with more than one person in it.*
> —MARY KARR

TEACHING OTHERS HOW TO TREAT YOU

At first, the concept of me teaching others how to treat me was both challenging and liberating. Challenging because, one, I was comfortable blaming others whom I felt treated me badly, and two, I didn't have a clue how to teach someone to treat me well. Growing up, I was taught how to treat others, but, as I recall, the subject of teaching them how to treat me wasn't mentioned. Thankfully, things are very different now. Kids are taught how to respect and honor others and are also shown how to insist on being treated well.

I felt liberated by the idea because it gave me the power of *choice*, inspired me to become more aware of what I wanted and needed, and pushed me to stand up for myself. Accepting I was in charge forced me to set limits and boundaries with family and friends and—the biggest stretch—have tough, honest conversations about behaviors that were unacceptable to me.

First and foremost, to teach others how to treat you well, you need to know you *deserve* to be treated well and actually *do it* for yourself. In other words, you need to "Do unto self as you would have others do unto you" before you are a convincing teacher. I know... the heart of the matter always seems to be self-love and self-compassion, doesn't it?

Teaching others how to treat you as you deserve to be treated can enliven and enrich many relationships. However, no matter how solidly you value yourself or how cleverly and compassionately you teach others, some people won't give a fig, others won't *want* to make changes, and others won't be *able* to provide what you request. It's still important to ask, but just because you know how to teach doesn't mean you will always get the results you want. When teaching doesn't work, you have other options. Do you want to continue the relationship, adapt to the parameters, or let it go?

There *are* nonnegotiables. For me to stay in any kind of relationship, respect and physical safety are requirements. You, undoubtedly, have nonnegotiables of your own.

Please know I'm not talking about domestic violence here. If you are in that situation, be a good friend to yourself and get help and find a safe place *now*.

During your day…

- ✧ Verbally assure yourself you deserve to be treated well.
- ✧ If you tend to be hard on yourself, notice when you're doing so and turn the dial to a gentler setting.
- ✧ Treat yourself as you wish others treated you.

> *You teach people how to treat you by what you allow, what you stop, and what you reinforce.*
>
> —TONY GASKINS

SAVING YOURSELF

Unlike the previous meditation on teaching people how to treat us, this one *is* about abusive relationships. I don't know what it is like to be in an abusive relationship. Although I've had clients who were caught in the tentacles of toxic relationships, the closest I've come to being directly involved was putting a client on a plane in Hawaii in order to keep her safe from a violent husband.

As I understand from clients, and three close friends who were abused wives, there are countless reasons that make it feel impossible to leave a cruel spouse. These women told me that freeing themselves from the tyranny of emotional manipulation and/or physical abuse required more strength than they thought they had, but they did it because they *had* to in order to survive emotionally and physically. Maybe the strength to save yourself is exactly what your soul is asking you for right now.

If you are in a relationship in which the only growth is that of *fear*—fear for yourself, fear for your children, fear of punishment—please do not try to continue alone. To survive, and eventually thrive, you need a circle of safety.

To get a sense of your options, it may be wise to call a hotline where professional abuse counselors can guide you to help. (Because a record of your call can be found by abusers, for your safety, make the call from a phone the abuser does not have access to.)

The National Domestic Violence Hotline is available 24/7 and is toll free:

✧ 1-800-799-7233 and 1-800-787-3224 for Deaf and Hearing Impaired

The Teen Dating Abuse Hotline is also available 24/7 and toll free:

✧ 1-866-331-9474 and 1-866-331-8453 for Deaf and Hearing Impaired

During your day...

✧ Please know you are lovable and I, and thousands of other women, are holding you in our hearts and praying for your safety and well-being.

You and your children, if you have them, deserve to be physically and emotionally safe.

BEING VISIBLE

We all long to be visible, especially to those we love and respect. If you've ever muttered to yourself, "Good grief, (*that person*) doesn't have a clue who I *really* am!" you are in good company. As touched on earlier, the yearnings of my own heart, and those of many of my clients, can be summed up in four short sentences: *See me. Hear me. Hold me. Feel with me.* Being seen, heard, held, and empathized with confirms we are known. Being known assuages a primal urge deep within our hearts to be connected and, therefore, safe.

The million dollar question is: Do you see, hear, hold, and feel with *yourself?*

Seeing, hearing, holding, and feeling with ourselves and others are relational, feminine qualities and the bedrock of a woman's strength and compassion. These qualities take time, attention, and empathy. Unfortunately, in today's mind-oriented and action-intense society, softer feminine qualities are easily overlooked—even in caring women.

One of the most valuable growth opportunities in the kiln of relationships is the realization that no one else's love and positive regard can take the place of self-love and self-respect. No one outside our skin has the power to make us visible to ourselves or to others. That is our soul's challenging playground.

Of course, being loved, seen, and known by others is life-enhancing, and we'll discuss that in the next meditation, "Choosing to Be Present." For now, it's all about you lovingly getting to know yourself more deeply. When I first uncovered my need for visibility and came up with the four imperatives—*See me. Hear me. Hold me. Feel with me*—I wrote them on three-by-five-inch cards and taped them on my mirror. It was actually fun to get better acquainted with the cool me. Not so much fun to know the petty, pissed-off, needy, vulnerable me. But those fragile and hurting parts of me were wounded child subpersonalities whom I could begin healing only when I knew they existed.

Wise women find strength in seeing themselves clearly and treating themselves compassionately.

During your day…

- ⬩ Rest in the embrace of the Sacred Feminine who will see, hear, hold, and feel with you.
- ⬩ Please, please be gentle with yourself on your journey of self-discovery. It's a lifelong process, and some days naturally feel more successful and loving than others.
- ⬩ Vulnerability and visibility go hand in hand. Both are evidence of strength.

> *Our deepest human need is not material at*
> *all: Our deepest need is to be seen.*
> —MARIANNE WILLIAMSON

CHOOSING TO BE PRESENT

I believe we want to satisfy the needs and longing of those we care about, really *see* them and intimately *know* them, but how do we actually know what their needs, delights, and longings are if we don't regularly choose to be completely present to them? The good news is most of us are suck-'em-up sponges when it comes to presence. Just a few minutes of eye-contact, full-attention, face-to-face concentration between friends or lovers or kids and parents can fill us to the brim. I think that's why having coffee or doing lunch is so popular—and necessary—for women. In those settings, we are *present* for each other in the moment. Texts and Snapchats are great for touching base but are not the satiating full-facial connecting of true presence.

Today, I was having a swear-a-thon hissy fit over a technical issue, and my hubby, Gene, was my captive audience. He lowered the paper, looked me square in the face, and just listened with a little smile. He chose to be absolutely present for about a minute and a half. I had been heard, seen, held in his gaze, and—it appeared—enjoyed. And it was enough. This full-minute-of-undivided-attention approach can also be magically effective with kids of all ages.

Speaking of kids, their gelled hairstyles have given new life to Brylcreem, so I've adapted Brylcreem's ancient jingle to... *"Presence: A little dab'll do ya!"*

Not always, of course, but often.

During your day…

✧ Choose to be completely present to yourself and one or
two other people, or pets, for a minute or two.

> *When you love someone, the best thing you can offer is*
> *your presence. How can you love if you are not there?*
> —THICH NHAT HANH

CLOSING THE CONDUIT

The romantic adage "opposites attract" often plays out in real-life
couples. One common pair of opposites is Emotional Expressers and
Emotional Suppressers. The danger in this relationship is that the
Expresser can easily become the guardian—and garbage collector—of
all the emotional energy generated in the partnership.

To picture an Expresser/Suppressor relationship, imagine the
couple as two cylinders side by side with a connecting conduit at
the bottom. Anything poured into one cylinder will flow through
the conduit and eventually fill both containers. As you can imagine,
Expressers clear their cylinders regularly by being aware of their feelings
and dealing with them. Expressers empty their trash. Suppressors often
don't even know they have trash and simply squash their feelings into
their containers until the energy is forced through the conduit into

their partner's cylinder. Without conscious awareness, an Expresser can begin carrying both her own and her partner's emotional energy. Because we Expressers are often caretakers, emptying our partner's trash can feel noble and helpful at first. But it quickly grows exhausting and frustrating.

If you feel tapped out, overloaded, used, or are being labeled "too emotional," you may be allowing your mate to stuff unresolved feelings and emotions in your personal cylinder. Time to close the conduit and handle only your own emotional/feeling energy. Take a moment to visualize the conduit between your two cylinders. Remove the conduit by whatever means comes to you and carefully patch the holes left in both containers. I put strong heart patches over mine. Thank the conduit for its work, and ask that its energy be transformed and transmuted into energy that is good for the Whole and release it to Source.

Be gentle with yourself and your mate if this scenario rings true for you. None of it was done maliciously or even consciously. Now that you know the pattern, you can change it. You can embrace the idea that loving your mate *is* your job, but taking out your mate's garbage or feeling *for* them is not.

A good way to start changing the pattern and closing the conduit is to stop trying to fix anything for your partner. Pay attention and be interested if they fume or ask for advice, but don't give it. As my teacher Mary Bell says, "I just say to my hubby, 'Hmmmm, that's interesting. I don't know what I'd do. What do you think?'"

Although I've used the metaphor of a romantic relationship here, the Expresser/Suppressor dynamic can also play out in other relationships.

During your day…

- ✧ Close or reclose any conduits bringing unwanted energy your way.
- ✧ Gently be aware of your own emotional energy and lovingly tend to it.

Own your own stuff and be careful not to step in someone else's.
—ROBIN ROBERTS

ACCEPTING RESPONSIBILITY

A sure sign of strength and maturity is the ability to accept responsibility for being at fault—but only when you actually *are* at fault. Unfortunately, after eons of training, women sometimes still feel obligated to take blame that isn't theirs in order to keep the peace, not "make mountains out of a molehills," smooth things over, protect someone's ego, or make things easier for the children. Certainly, this kind of behavior creates a relationship kiln, but not one that is strengthening, creates beauty, or inspires growth. Although some partners may allow another to take responsibility for their mistakes in order to save face, that decision undermines both the relationship and the people in it.

If you are choosing to take unwarranted responsibility, or are in a relationship with someone who needs to be right all the time and casts blame on you, how do you feel? Strong and empowered does not spring to my mind. When you are hurt and the person responsible refuses to admit fault or, even worse, tries to make it your fault, how does that feel? In such situations, I feel frustrated, dismissed, angry, sad, less trusting, and more defensive. Resentments mushroom and relationships flounder when only one person is capable of culpability. When both people are willing to be accountable, things can usually be worked out. As therapist and author Rick Hanson says, "When someone admits fault to me, I feel safer, on more solid ground, more at ease, warmer toward them and more willing to admit faults myself."

If you are one who has an inordinate need to be right, it would be wise to question what insecurities and vulnerabilities may be hiding behind that necessity. To come into your full strength and empowerment, gently explore the underlying feelings causing you to resist taking responsibility for being at fault. Awareness provides insight that can open a path toward healing.

A word of caution: If you fear for your safety in a relationship and feel compelled to accept blame in order to prevent emotional or physical abuse, I urge you to seek help. Please don't try to go it alone.

Accepting and taking responsibility for your fair share show strength, maturity, and self-confidence.

During your day...

- ✧ Without judgment, pause and reflect on your feelings if you want to dodge taking responsibility for your actions.
- ✧ Do the same if you are aware of wanting to take unwarranted responsibility.
- ✧ Be gentle and compassionate with yourself, especially while teetering on a growing edge.

A mistake is simply another way of doing things.
—E. B. WHITE

BEING GENEROUS WITH EXPRESSIONS OF LOVE

A little saying I try to live by is "Nice wears well." When younger and motivated mostly by fear, I used to cringe when someone called me nice or sweet because those two descriptors felt like polite alternatives for weak and wussy. In reality, my only weakness when acting nice was the fear and consternation I felt if I received a negative response or no response at all. Although genuine, my niceness really *needed* a positive response and, therefore, was not a gift but a bit of pleasant bartering. To be authentically nice and sweet, I needed to be comfortable enough in my own skin to give up wanting any kind of response and express love, endearments, and appreciations simply because it brought *me* joy.

As fear of offending anyone gave up its grip and the art of being myself became more natural, my heart opened and I found myself having a lot of fun generously expressing love and delight in people. It helps that I am literally a little ol' lady in tennis shoes because enjoying tremendous leeway in terms of behavior is one of the perks of Elderdom.

Once after expressing a now-forgotten bit of love or appreciation, the little ditty "Stop expecting tit for tat. Love just because that's where it's at" danced through my mind. It was so silly and sassy, the bad grammar didn't even bug me. That little rhyme totally nailed why I felt the freedom to express as I did. Tit for tat was not an issue anymore. I was just having a grand time expressing feelings in the moment, and no response was needed.

For the most part, people love being the recipient of any kind of positive regard, yet out of fear, we can be very guarded with our words and actions. I encourage you to open up your heart spigot and give yourself permission to become more generous with expressions of love and positivity. I wish I'd had the strength and wisdom to shower compliments, gold stars, and way-to-gos much earlier. But, truly, it's never too late nor too soon. Go for it; you'll love it. And so will most of the recipients, I bet.

During your day...

- ✧ Allow yourself a little more freedom of expression.
- ✧ If it feels right to you, give yourself the challenge of complimenting one or two people a day.
- ✧ Say "I love you" more often. Choose at least one new recipient a week.

Expressing love and appreciation helps you feel more of each.

OPTING FOR FREQUENT FORGIVENESS

Forgiveness is a liberating habit to embrace. Although forgiveness seems like something we give others, it's actually a gift of freedom we bestow upon ourselves.

A few years ago, I took a series of classes studying the Lord's Prayer in Aramaic, the language in which Jesus taught it. To this day, in my mangled version of Aramaic, I recite or sing the prayer to comfort or uplift myself. One of the things that struck me about the original prayer was how softly, yet powerfully, kind and understanding it was. For instance, the Aramaic word for forgive is *cancel* and forgiveness is defined as canceling all demands, conditions, and expectations that prevent the mind from maintaining an attitude of love.

As I understand this definition, forgiving, or canceling, allows the flow of love and positive regard to move freely through us even when we're hurt or angry. In a close relationship—with another or ourselves—instead of blaming, shaming, or withdrawing, we accept the fact that we're human and are going to make mistakes, while still honoring our feelings in the moment. With that openhearted and accepting attitude, we can honestly say something akin to "I'm hurt and not feeling warm and fuzzy toward you right now, but I forgive you, and we'll be okay."

To be clear, canceling isn't the same as condoning or approving. It doesn't negate or deny wrongdoing. But it does remove the *requirement* that you, or another, must perform in a certain way in order to be deserving of love. Of course, while forgiving is always freeing for the forgiver, it doesn't mean you need to maintain relationships with those whom you forgive. You can forgive *impersonally* and for the purpose of keeping your life force flowing. You can wish others well *and* choose never to see them again.

Because nonforgiveness acts as a freezing agent, locked in its judgmental jaws, nothing can change. Because forgiveness flows, in its presence, love grows and miracles can occur.

During your day...

- ✧ Forgive yourself for everything, big and small.
- ✧ Know that accountability and forgiveness do not cancel each other out.
- ✧ We are human and will need to forgive and be forgiven time and again.

True forgiveness is when you can say,
"Thank you for that experience."

—OPRAH WINFREY

5

ACKNOWLEDGING AND HEALING WOUNDS

Healing wounds and claiming truth
is the crux of the matter for everybody,
whether they realize it or not.

—Patricia Sun

As uncomfortable as it can be, being able to acknowledge and accept your wounds is usually the best way to heal them. What is brought into the open can be healed, whereas hurts and distresses left buried in the deep caverns of the unconscious mind tend to grow unchecked and emerge in unhealthy ways such as illness, anxiety, or depression.

Awareness is the first step on any healing path because we can bring something into the open only when we are aware of its existence. You may be wondering why not let sleeping dogs lie: if you don't know it's there, then leave it alone. And, it's true, if a wound is dormant and not causing any distress, fear, or limitation, it's wise to let it be. However, if you are experiencing symptoms of dis-ease in any form—physical, emotional, mental, relational, or spiritual—more than likely there is a healing opportunity awaiting your attention.

The most important aspect of any healing effort is to honor your unique process. Your healing method may be straightforward and someone else's more circuitous and subtle. For instance, in my counseling practice, a couple of times I was pretty sure a client had been sexually abused in childhood. But if the client didn't mention any abuse, neither did I. First, because I could have been wrong and, second, because there are very effective ways to heal without knowing the details of any given scenario. Essentially, it is feelings that need healing, not events.

CRADLING A HURTING HEART

Our hearts are vast beyond comprehension and, yes, vulnerable and easily hurt. Today, my heart is steadfastly doing it's life-sustaining work while also busily balancing an array of emotions. Due to grief, concern, and sadness, my heart is in need of a little gentle kindness. Yours may feel similarly much of the time.

Self-supportive attitudes are essential for cradling hurting hearts. I often use the following three attitudes to help soothe and mend my heart.

AWARENESS—BRING BENEVOLENT AND GENTLE INTEREST TO INNER EXPLORATION

Awareness is the first step toward healing. What is known can be transformed. In a warm, protected cradle of benevolent and gentle interest, our hearts can safely explore vulnerabilities, wounds, and struggles as well as insights, triumphs, and joys. Awareness and exploration help you understand your feelings. Understanding provides insight into what might be healing and helpful for your aching heart, and also keeps you from projecting misunderstood feelings onto others, which, by itself, is conducive to a happier heart.

ACCEPTANCE—ALLOW THIS MOMENT'S FEELINGS

For much of my life, *resistance* and its kissing cousins *blame* and *shame* (BS for short) were knee-jerk reactions to difficult feelings and circumstances. Thankfully, age and experience have taught me that resistance and BS magnify, rather than diminish, pain and I can usually choose to embrace the feminine energy of acceptance. Becoming more skilled in the art of acceptance is surprisingly strengthening and has also increased my peace of mind immensely. Hurting hearts are more apt to transform pain into compassion, understanding, and wisdom when cradled in the soft embrace of acceptance.

AWE AND AMUSEMENT—NOTICE BOTH THE FANTASTIC AND FUNNY

Almost any situation has the possibility of either awe or amusement in it when we are able to consider that option. Recently, I heard an interview with an author whose memoir included her cancer journey. The author shared she made it a point to look for heartening moments during chemo treatments. One day she observed an elderly gentleman gently moving a wisp of hair from his wife's eye. Seeing that glimpse of long-term love lifted her heart and brought a smile to her face. I remember a similar moment. Riding in the mortuary's family car on the way to my mother's burial, my dad pointed out the window at a foal and its mother. Baby was exuberantly kicking up her heels as mom looked on with what I saw as delight. Thirty years down the road, that sweet moment is one of my clearest memories from of that day.

During your day...

⋄ If your heart is hurting, treat it as a loving, delighted, and indulgent mother would.

⋄ Live gently with your own and others' hearts.

Our sorrows and wounds are healed only
when we touch them with compassion.

—BUDDHA

FACING AND EMBRACING

Pain has a bad reputation. Our instinct is to avoid it, resist it, and downplay it with the hope it will disappear. It doesn't. In reality, pain is a master teacher to your soul. Without it, you would not be as compassionate, wise, or strong. Your best source of understanding, transformation, and growth is the exploration and healing of pain.

I grant you, pain hurts. It was the excruciating pain ignited by the failure of my first marriage that forced me to face and embrace aspects of myself I didn't even know existed. Believe me, I resisted what pain had to offer because the feelings were so tsunami-like. I was afraid I'd be washed away, annihilated by anger, and irreparably broken by grief. But I sold myself short, as we often do, because I emerged—with *a lot* of help from friends and teachers, two young sons, a dog, a kitten, and a bunny—infinitely stronger, more compassionate, and confident in my ability to learn from future pain and sorrow. From that experience, I can vouch for Kahlil Gibran's teaching "Your pain is the breaking of the shell that encloses your understanding."

Understanding and transformation can develop as you:

- ✧ **Invite assistance**: When pain is intense, you typically need help and guidance to move through it constructively. Assistance comes in myriad forms. Humans, angels, God, your own imagination, therapists, support groups, whatever or whoever feels supportive and nurturing to you.

✧ **Face**: Gather your courage—you are far more courageous than you feel!—and turn to meet your pain. Small glimpses at a time are fine.

✧ **Explore**: Become curious. Curiosity neutralizes resistance and defuses fear. Getting to know something renders it less frightening. Name it. Notice what it looks like. Is there a subpersonality that embodies this pain? If so, gently and nonjudgmentally become acquainted.

✧ **Embrace**: Greet your pain. "Hi! I recognize you. What have you got to teach me this time?" Fill your heart with acceptance and embrace your pain as is. It's okay to fake it till you feel it. Just set an *intention* to embrace and accept until you actually accomplish it.

Embracing and accepting pain as a wise and loving mentor allow its energy to transform and flow into healing and resolution.

During your day…

✧ If need be, entertain the idea of viewing pain differently.

⟡ If pain is too scary to face right now, shrink it to the size
    of a lucky penny and carry it in your pocket until you
    are able to face it.

Facing and embracing are transformative and empowering.

ENCOURAGING EXPRESSION

Twenty years ago I had the profound honor of being in the birthing room supporting a first-time mom-to-be. Labor had been long and intense, and the young woman was beyond exhaustion. Until hearing it was too late for an epidural, Mom had been stoic and quiet, but shoved to the brink as pushing began, she started making appropriate sounds and voicing fears that she couldn't go on. Her husband was unfailingly encouraging and supportive, but the doctor—a woman, I'm ashamed to say—told her to stop yelling (which she wasn't) and declared all that noise didn't help (which wasn't much and very well could have helped release pent-up energy). Shocked and incensed, I told the mother to make whatever noise she needed to, but she was successfully silenced by "authority." Until she cried with happiness when her healthy son was given to her, this valiant new mom did not utter another word.

What the less-than-compassionate doctor didn't seem to know is that expression is essential. Pent-up emotion needs outlets. Unexpressed toxic energy lodges in our cells and can create dis-ease of many kinds. If you feel the need "to put a sock in it," as a Texan friend says, please give yourself permission to express freely... but safely. I am not talking about expression that puts you in harm's way or is unloving or inappropriate, like making a mother-bashing wedding toast. I'm encouraging *healthy, cathartic*, mostly private expression that can include sobbing or laughing, private shouts and swears that give voice to new and ancient griefs. Physical exertion such as shouting "NO!" as you hit a bed with a tennis racket is also a great way to get energy moving.

Personally and with clients, I've used throwing eggs at trees, punching a body bag, hitting telephone books with a rubber hose, and, of course, the old standby—screaming and shouting in the privacy of my own house. I find each of these methods helpful, safe, and satisfying outlets for pent-up energy. There are countless ways to express effectively and constructively, and I'm sure you have some of your own.

During your day...

✦ If you need to express feelings, give yourself permission to do so in ways that make you feel good about yourself.

✦ Let it out!

Trust your feelings and urges. Energy doesn't lie.

TAKING A BREAK

The human nervous system is miraculous, almost unbelievably complex and capable. And, like any other functioning entity, your nervous system needs to take an occasional break to rest and recharge. As a result of unrelenting sensory stimulation, our own inner expectations, and super-stuffed schedules, our valiant nervous systems operate at red alert much of the time. For it to stay healthy, your nervous system needs to take breaks from hyperactivity and hypervigilance.

Sleep is important, and small "offline" time-outs during the day are also necessary to nourish and restore body, mind, and nerves.

Engaging your imagination is also a wonderful way to create short, relaxing time-outs. To begin, let your eyes drift closed and become aware of your breathing. No need to change it; just observe your breath with gratitude. After several inhales and exhales, move your awareness to your nervous system and allow an image of it to arise in your mind's eye. It's okay to focus solely on your spinal cord, knowing it disperses energy to the entire body automagically. How would you describe the energy of your nervous system right now? What color is it? Does that color feel calm and restful? If not, allow a soothing, calming color to appear. Surround and saturate your spinal column with the color. When I was doing this exercise the other day, my spinal cord first appeared to be a throbbing red. I chose to cool it down with Bimini blue, a Caribbean ocean color that is peaceful to me.

Because there is construction and discombobulating noise pollution around our home, I bathe my nervous system in Bimini blue often. Another little practice I do when my nervous system is shouting out red alerts such as *"There's not enough time! You can't do this! It's impossible!"* is imagine a beautiful big bubble—like kids blow with little wands—in front of me. Into it, I put dire red alert warnings plus fears, anxieties, or doubts that are nagging at me. With the help of angels, I let the bubble float away. My imagination loves angels, but yours may conjure up other imagery that resonates with your soul. The purpose of these practices is to cool and calm your nervous system with loving attention and a bit of oasis time and space.

During your day...

❖ Take mini-rest-cations just for the health of it.
❖ Soothe your nervous system with color.

> *Maybe the most important teaching is to*
> *lighten up and relax.*
> —PEMA CHÖDRÖN

GROWING THROUGH GRIEF

Grief is inevitable. Growing through grief is a choice.

When grief is fresh, our thoughts rarely turn to the idea of what grief has to teach us. No, in the beginning hours, days, and especially nights, of grief, taking the next breath is sometimes all we have energy for. Early stages of grief can include disbelief, terror, rage, temporary collapse, inability to think clearly, and helplessness, plus innumerable other overwhelming feelings. During times of intense loss and grief, please be gentle with yourself, cradle your gasping heart, and allow others to help you.

Because we are incredibly resilient beings, healing ultimately begins to touch our hearts and souls. Numbness ebbs into awareness, fury cools to anger, and our brains falteringly creep from their caves. Cautiously, you are turning your face toward life as it is now. This is the time you may fleetingly wonder what you can learn from this anguish. The idea of how you might help others going through similar trauma may also begin to germinate in the depths of your consciousness.

As a therapist and facilitator of hospice grief support groups, I have seen a lot of grief and, of course, experienced my share. Not all, but most women come through loss and grief—whether from death, divorce, war, betrayal, abuse, disillusionment—with their hearts broken *open*, not shattered beyond repair. They have gone through fire and emerged more deeply attuned to themselves and others, ripped open only to discover increased compassion, empathy, and understanding.

It appears woman are experts at gleaning growth as the vast majority of us grow more able to love under the tutelage of grief.

During your day...

+ Tuck the idea of growing through grief into a soft corner of your heart to be retrieved when needed.
+ Love and accept yourself unconditionally during times of loss and grief. Doing so probably won't be easy, but will definitely facilitate healing.

> *The difficulties of our lives can soften us, make us kinder to each other and more compassionate.*
> —PEMA CHÖDRÖN

REVISING OUR STORIES

Because parents are human, very few of us had completely idyllic childhoods. Less-than-ideal experiences usually provide growth opportunities that assist our development. However, when feelings evoked by childhood experiences haunt us into adulthood, healing is called for. In my twenties, before I knew beans about psychology or metaphysics, Annabelle—who would become my spiritual mother and mentor—helped me overcome lingering pain from a childhood memory through a visualization she called "grafting a new childhood." My ignorant—I say that with affection—twentysomething self was highly skeptical.

Annabelle guided me through revising a story I'd created about a particularly hurtful incident and helped me craft a happy ending. Much to my amazement, I felt better. Who knows, maybe that was the first baby step on an eventual career path.

Your subconscious mind believes what you tell it, especially when the narrative is accompanied by feeling (the more intense, the deeper the belief). Feeling-energy becomes truth to the subconscious mind. Because it has no capacity to edit, like a trusting child, your subconscious absorbs whatever you provide. Since feeling-energy is the result of thoughts, and thoughts are gathered into stories, it behooves us to imbue our stories with uplifting energy.

Take a moment to think of a story you're telling yourself. It can be something weighty from childhood or a simpler story such as "I bet they think I was awful to say ___ yesterday!" Immerse yourself in the story. After a couple of minutes, notice what you are feeling. If the feelings aren't great, create a new story. A feel-good one. Outlandish is A-OK, and you as the heroine is recommended. After musing on the new story for a while, notice your feelings again. If you find yourself stuck in the concepts of "truth or reality," remember, if reimaging events transforms the energy of difficult emotions, who cares what "reality" is/was/may be? If changing your story allows painful energy to dissipate or transform into positive uplifting feelings, mission accomplished!

During your day...

✦ Inner stories create feelings. Choose to revise pain-provoking stories into ones that generate happier, more self-supportive feelings.

✦ Treat yourself to a few fairytale endings.

> *What happens is of little significance compared with the stories we tell ourselves about what happens. Events matter little, only stories of events affect us.*
>
> —RABIH ALAMEDDINE

IMBUING PAIN WITH PURPOSE

In joy, we are blessed and, through sorrow, we have the opportunity to become blessings. Because we've *been* there, *felt* that, we can understand and empathize with the heartache of others. Having endured and grown through the agony of loss and the despair of injustice, we can bring compassion and presence to those in the grip of pain.

Being able to hold someone's hand and listen with an understanding heart brings purpose to pain even though we have no way of knowing how meaningful those momentary connections may be to the recipient. I personally can't imagine understanding and empathy ever being anything other than comforting.

Some people use their pain as fuel for creating greater good through large organizations such as Mothers Against Drunk Driving (MADD), changing laws concerning dangerous traditions like fraternity hazing; and the #MeToo movement with its motto of Empowerment Through Empathy. Most of us, however, will imbue pain with purpose in smaller ways.

When my two sons were in their late teens, within a few days of each other, both experienced life-changing events. Brett, my youngest who had dreams of being a professional soccer player, blew out his kicking knee. A local surgeon warned he might never walk again without a limp. Less than a week later, Mike, my oldest whose ambition was acting, contracted Bell's palsy and half his face was paralyzed. My mother-heart was as shattered as my sons' dreams for the future. It wasn't until both boys were recovering from surgery (Brett) and treatment (Mike) that I thought of imbuing my pain with purpose. When I remembered, I prayed that this pain eventually allow me to help and understand others more deeply. This week, I've been keeping in touch with a neighbor whose fourteen-year-old daughter had open-heart surgery two days ago. She says my empathy and prayers are comforting.

Sometimes the purpose of our pain is completely personal: to make us stronger, increase patience, wake up to a new direction, make us kinder or more accepting. Ask your wise intuition to reveal the purpose of your pain. Be patient; answers often come more slowly than we'd like.

During your day…

- ⟡ Honor your pain through treating yourself gently
  and lovingly.
- ⟡ Allow pain to work its magic on your heart and soul.

Pain teaches lessons no scholar can.
—KAMAHL

LIGHTING UP AND LETTING FLOW

As a result of being deeply attuned to ourselves and others, it is also natural to feel pain deeply. A couple of wonderful leavening agents for pain are light and flow.

To lessen intensity and invite healing, first pay complete, nonjudgmental attention to an emotional or physical pain and encourage it to show itself to you. Imagine, or "see," what it looks like. Color, texture, size, shape? Now envision what the pain feels like. Huge, overwhelming, dense, fearful, heavy, sharp? For a few moments, simply *allow* the pain. Be curious and remain as neutral as possible.

Because you are paying close attention, this simple exercise is often helpful by itself. But, as an added boost, we'll add light. With continuing curiosity, surround and saturate the pain with light. Either colored or clear light is fine. As the pain laps up light enthusiastically, see if you can catch a glimpse of grace or recognize a wisp of wisdom in the cause of your pain. If not, that's okay. If it feels right, imagine a beautiful source of light far, far away and ask the pain if it would be willing to be absorbed by that light. If it refuses, ask it what it wants and needs from you right now.

Winston Churchill said, "If you're going through hell, keep going." This brings us to the idea of flow. When hellish energy of any kind is holed up inside you, let it flow. My friend Mary Bell teaches students to create a grounding cord, as wide as their hips, from the base of the spine to the center of Mother Earth. A grounding cord can take many forms; mine has appeared as a curvy red dragon tail, a thick tree root, a cement truck slide, and a crystal channel. Anchor your grounding cord into place at the center of the Earth and effortlessly allow feelings and energy to flow freely down it. Your center will undoubtedly be different, but I envision mine as a Cavern of Transformation in which my offerings are transformed and transmuted into energy that is good for the whole.

Please be patient and gentle with yourself as you dissipate pain. The process can take longer than we instant-result enthusiasts like.

During your day…

⋄ Give yourself a new grounding cord each day. It only takes seconds to imagine what today's grounding cord looks like. A grounding cord may appear the same each day or take on a new look according to your mood and need. When I'm feeling vulnerable, my grounding cord often resembles a redwood tree. When I'm feeling lighthearted, it may become a dragon's tail or channel of light. Effortlessly allow unwanted energy to be released from your body and psyche by flowing down your grounding cord into the center of Mother Earth.

✧ Bathe yourself and any current pain in the soothing balm of beautiful light.

> *There are two ways of spreading light:*
> *to be the candle or the mirror that reflects it.*
>
> —EDITH WHARTON

TURNING SCARS TO STARS

Gracie, a friend, whom I call the Empress of Empathy, told me her mother had hated her. Since hateful energy is often self-hatred projected onto an innocent target, this appears to be what happened to Gracie. Mom got pregnant and married—in that order—before she was ready to and, instead of owning and working with her feelings, projected them onto an innocent baby who didn't ask to be born. In doing so, Gracie's mother kept her scars fresh and created new ones in the next generation. I was saddened but inspired to hear that Gracie, a universally loved and respected woman, had overcome such a searing wound to become an absolute star at making others feel loved and valued. She assured me she'd had plenty of dicey times and she'd been working on many scars for decades and continued to work on them when needed. Her ability to turn scars into stars came with the help of insightful therapists, important teachers, God, meaningful work, the support of other family members and friends, plus her own determination to heal, be happy, and help others be happy also.

As I mused about Gracie's story, it became clear to me that turning scars to stars is a strength women use daily. We transform our scars by owning and honoring them long before they become star-worthy. We grow from the lessons scars provide and become better people in the process. Through sharing our stories and revealing our vulnerabilities, we not only receive the support and guidance we need, but model how important authenticity, honesty, and sharing are to empowerment and healing.

When we can embrace Anaïs Nin's belief "The scar meant that I was stronger than what had tried to hurt me," we are well on the way to creating a star-studded life while, at the same time, making the night sky brighter for others through our courage.

During your day…

✧ Dare to embrace and honor your scars.
✧ Soothe unhealed scars with the balm of awareness and discerning exposure.

Everyone alive participates in this human cycle of build and mend. It's how the Universe keeps growing. While each disappointment feels so large, so destructive, falling and getting up is the exercise by which the muscle of life breaks itself down in order to get stronger.

—MARK NEPO

6

EXPANDING AWARENESS

*Awareness is like the sun. When it shines
on things, they are transformed.*
—Thich Nhat Hanh

Awareness is the key to strength. In fact, it's the key to just about everything that gives life zing and meaning. Awareness brings us into the here and now, allowing us to savor and participate wholly in *this moment*, the only moment we are truly alive.

Outer awareness is a wonderful way to stay in the present moment. Being aware of our surroundings prompts appreciation for the beauty and majesty around us. Awareness helps us tune in to the people crossing our paths who enhance our lives or—in some cases—offer excellent growth opportunities. Nuanced awareness lends itself to mindfulness and gratitude practice. Noticing what is happening, in any given moment, grounds and centers us in the here and now.

Inner awareness provides the same benefits as outer awareness while adding pizazz and depth (as well as dismay and chagrin on occasion). Since you are an audience of one for what is dancing or drudging in the theater of your mind, inner awareness is a never-ending source of private amusement. Well, let's put it this way, inner awareness *better* be a source of amusement because interior insights and discoveries run the gamut from shiny gold encrusted nuggets of wisdom to actions and attitudes suitable only for the nearest cesspool.

Awareness is the first step toward inner and outer change. I invite you to enjoy your explorations by entering this chapter with unconditional friendlessness toward yourself (thank you, Pema), a thoughtful interest in your inner and outer realms, and your sense of humor close at hand.

ELEVATING ATTITUDE

Attitude affects everything. It colors every feeling, experience, chore, triumph, thought, creation, and relationship—especially the one with yourself. Attitude is like an omnipresent dye, tinting or tainting each thread in the fabric of your being. Awareness is an early warning signal alerting you to the need for a change in attitude. Unless afflicted with mental illness or a brain-chemical imbalance, we are the creators and guardians of our attitudes and, therefore, can change them when appropriate.

I've found that elevating my attitude is the epitome of self-compassion and also positively affects how strong and competent I feel. If my attitude has curdled, I don't feel like being compassionate to anyone, especially me. When my compassion quotient is low, I see myself as a "bad" person, which, in turn, makes me feel weak and ineffectual. So, the best thing I can do for myself is to become aware of my underlying attitude. For instance, not that long ago, I succumbed to heavy resistance to several personal and public circumstances beyond my control. As often happens when I'm writing a new book, I became my own *bad* example. My attitude soured and scraped bottom and, instead of being self-compassionate, I berated myself for being an ingrate.

That attitude persisted for longer than I care to remember, but eventually I calmed down enough to do the internal work necessary. The underlying beliefs causing my rock-bottom attitude were twofold. I felt powerless and victimized. With that awareness, I began to hoist myself out of the hole by being diligent in changing my thoughts, but most importantly, treating myself kindly. I found my subpersonality who carried the majority of the powerless victimized feelings and loved and accepted—in lieu of shaming—her back to balance and strength. I also concentrated on what I *could* do, educating myself and making changes wherever possible. The help of many caring people supported and blessed me as I grappled with these feelings. As you've probably guessed, this is a condensed version of the process because elevating attitude and restoring self-compassion usually take time and patience.

During your day…

- ✧ Be aware of your attitude, lightening and elevating it as soon as possible.
- ✧ If your attitude loses altitude, gently uncover the underlying beliefs causing its spiral.
- ✧ Know you deserve, and thrive on, self-compassion no matter how you feel.

*Enduring strength is protected by an attitude
of self-compassion and kindness.*

PLAYING YOUR PART TO THE HILT

Have you ever felt "All the world's a stage," as Shakespeare said, yet you were only cast in bit parts? There are those who think it is their job to be the director of your life and decide what parts you'll play and what parts are forbidden, but they're wrong. You are author, director, producer, and player of your life story. Those who ask you to dim your light because it hurts their eyes need to wear sunglasses, and those who want you to stay out of the spotlight need to learn to share.

While entities such as the patriarchy want us to stay small, our souls have hopes and dreams for us that include learning and growing by playing our roles to the hilt. As souls incarnated in female bodies, women are being called to bring heart- and relationship-centered feminine qualities front and center. Many women who have decided to stop playing small—or never felt the need to—are embodying the energy of love, inclusion, and wisdom as they take their rightful places beside others in the spotlight. For the good of the entire world, center stage is being balanced with a more feminine presence.

Please know I'm not talking about us becoming divas and taking over the world burlesque fashion. By taking center stage and being in the spotlight, I am referring to us enhancing our lives and society by speaking our truth, acting authentically, and sharing our wisdom privately and publicly.

I hope you are among the many women who naturally play their part to the hilt, as family lore says I did as a little girl. I only vaguely remember that me. After the birth of my sister when I was seven, I mostly recall feeling the need to play small, a feeling that persisted well into adulthood. Let's meet *your* child self: gently close your eyes and notice your breath for a minute. Allow an image of you as a little girl to float into your mind's eye. In whatever way feels right to you, get better acquainted with her. Does she have permission to be herself, to speak up, and be what she feels is right even if others disagree? If not, can you give her permission to play her part to the hilt now and throughout the rest of your shared life?

During your day...

✦ Stay in touch with your inner little girl. Over time, you will probably have much wisdom and love to share.

Take center stage and play your life's parts with
awareness, amusement, and abandon.

GATHERING GLIMPSES OF GOOD

Like a doting fairy godmother, the universe is continually providing opportunities for us to gather glimpses of good. Some, like heart-shaped clouds, are fleeting while others, such as the kindness of friends, are more steadfast. Each glimpse of goodness you are aware of, and register as "good," causes your brain to spit out mood-elevating endorphins.

It's especially wise to gather glimpses of good during times when reality is tough to handle. Several years ago, half our house was destroyed in a flood. Daily we were blessed by glimpses of good from total strangers as well as friends and family. Girl Scout troops and church groups brought lunches to our door (with gluten-free options, even!). Neighbors who hadn't been affected also brought food and let us shower in their homes. Volunteers and dayworkers plunged into our mud-filled downstairs rescuing what they could and dragging the unsalvageable to the mountain of detritus growing in the street. The memory of everyone's kindness brings tears to my eyes as I write this.

While much goodness was people-centered, there was one Universe-orchestrated sight I'll never forget. A few days into the cleanup process, the mud had began to harden, and in our devastated cul-de-sac, standing upright in the middle of a mud heap was a single dirty, but unbroken, light bulb. Hard to miss the message of that whimsical visual. And it provided a great photo op as well as a good laugh.

Another bonus of gathering glimpses of goodness close to your heart is they can be replayed. Like mini feel-good movies, glimpses can be reseen and, very importantly, refelt whenever you like.

Interestingly, the more supported we feel by the universe, the stronger we can be.

Toward that end, awareness allows us to see, appreciate, and take personally encouraging messages that seem to be saying, *"We are here… way to go, girl!"*

During your day…

- ✧ Be aware of at least one message from your fairy godmother or the Universe.
- ✧ Give your brain the chance to douse you with endorphins by opening your eyes and heart to the angelic ruffling of feathers, stirred by people, pets, or (possibly) leprechauns.

The universe is always speaking to us.
Sending us little messages, causing coincidences and
serendipities, reminding us to stop, to look around,
to believe in something else, something more.

—NANCY THAYER

QUESTIONING OVER-BUSYNESS

I think over-busyness is a soft addiction afflicting much of our society. There are myriad reasons why we drive, overschedule, and overcommit ourselves; some are societal, family, and personal expectations; private goals; and maybe some fear of not doing or being enough. Some busyness is probably simply ingrained habit. What led me to the idea of busyness being a soft addiction was the one reason I haven't heard mentioned much. Busyness has a numbing effect, as does addiction. No matter what form or substance it includes, addiction is used to numb emotional, spiritual, or physical pain and fear. Or a combination of those. Are we busily numbing ourselves or running away from something we fear?

I believe the major spiritual reason we have taken human form is to know ourselves inside and out and love ourselves unconditionally no matter what we discover. In other words, we are here to become as goddess-like as possible. What if that scares the @#!%*# out of us? What if at least a little of our busyness is a way to avoid knowing ourselves? What if we fear what we'll find... or that we'll not measure up... or be expected to take on too much responsibility as a result... or _____ (whatever else may spring to your mind)?

Aristotle assures us that "Knowing yourself is the beginning of all wisdom," but what if, deep down, we doubt we're capable of wisdom? What if, deeper still, we don't *want* to know ourselves because we don't like what we already see?

This subject is a muse-in-progress so I have no answers, just a gut feeling and a little experience. I *feel* as if we were created as wise, loving, and lovable beings and don't need to worry about that. I *experience* loving myself more deeply as I grow to know and understand myself more intimately.

During your day...

- ✧ If you are uncomfortably busy, muse about why.
- ✧ Courageously, but gently, ask yourself, "What if_____?" and allow intuition to fill in the blank.
- ✧ Notice if the amount of busyness you live with increases your strength or saps it.

It's not so much how busy you are,
*but **why** you are busy. The bee is praised.*
The mosquito is swatted.

—MARY O'CONNOR

EDITING INNER STORIES

Left unedited, many stories we tell ourselves sabotage our strength and happiness. Most of us have rich and powerful inner lives, when awake *and* asleep. Dreams are nighttime stories lush with symbology and chock-full of insights but often hard to remember and even tougher to interrupt. Daytime stories are less convoluted but often so deeply embedded in self-created mythology that we can no longer tell fact from fiction.

Recently, I caught myself rehashing an inner story that badly needed editing. I was working in the kitchen, and Gene was reading the paper at the table. He chuckled, and I was immediately as irritated as a PMS porcupine. After I muttered to myself for a few ultra-annoyed moments, awareness tapped me on the shoulder and woke me to reality. As many couples do, we have some issues with communication, and the story I was immersed in was built around a litany of communication complaints. In this story, I was cast as the person who always initiated and facilitated communication, and Gene was the character who *knowingly* tantalized me—a very curious person—with unexplained chuckles and exclamations. My character was obligated to inquire what was funny and, damn it, I was sick of the role. As a result of this long-ago concocted story, my internal dialog was heavy on judgmental "He did… and he doesn't…," and I was getting madder by the minute. Throughout my entire inner drama, Gene was simply reading the paper.

Although often *not* the case, this time awareness brought with it instant amusement, and I commented to myself, "Well, *that* was fun...." " Nope, not really. So what do I want to do with this story? For starters, label it fiction.

When you find yourself overreacting, chances are a dog-eared inner fable is replaying. During those times, the following questions can be helpful:

1. What story am I telling myself right now?
2. Am I more loving because of this story?
3. Does this tale make me happy?
4. How do I want to edit this story?

Be gentle with the author of your inner narratives. Congratulate her on her creativity, be amused by her mind's antics, and encourage her to craft uplifting stories casting herself as a strong, wise, and entertaining woman.

During your day...

- ✧ With gentle humor, become aware of inner stories.
- ✧ If you want, edit stories in ways that bring more balance and harmony into your life.

Live the story you want to tell.
—SIMPLY TOPAZ

LISTENING TO BODY WISDOM

Our bodies carry the wisdom of the ancients and the ages within their DNA. Our physical bodies are vast resources of original instinct and intuition, yet we seldom truly listen to them. Bodies are excellent barometers of our personal emotions as well as the emotional climate of people and situations we encounter. When we pay attention, our bodies alert us to people to avoid, situations to ignore, and on rare occasions, danger that can be avoided. We've all heard sayings such as "I felt like I'd been kicked in the gut," or "For no apparent reason, the hairs on the back of my neck stood up," or "Walking into that office felt like being hit with a two-by-four," or "As soon as we were introduced, my throat closed down." While some bodily reactions are unconscious projections, most are not, and therefore it's important to pay attention when strong reactions arise.

Several years ago, I was going to the office of a woman with whom I was working on a church project. I'd met her but didn't know her. She had said it was okay to bring my little dog along because her two dogs liked company. The entire drive over, I was aware of feeling queasy but didn't really pay attention. Not long after we arrived, one of her dogs attacked my dog, Lily, and scared both of us out of our wits. The owner of the attacking dog acted as if it was Lily's fault and was so rude that I was experiencing full-blown nausea by the time I left the office. My wise body somehow knew this experience was not going to be a good one, and I ignored it. Lily and I are both lucky the price of my blasé attitude was as minimal as it was.

Strong, powerful women use all the resources presented to them. By honoring our bodies as the wise sages they are, we make a trustworthy and reliable friend for our entire life's journey. Appreciating, accepting, caring for, and *listening* to your body are among the wisest choices you can make.

During your day…

✧ Listen to the sage in whom your soul resides.

> *There is more wisdom in your body than in your deepest philosophy.*
> —FRIEDRICH NIETZSCHE

PROMOTING INNER PEACE

I absolutely believe inner peace is possible—even probable—as we become *aware* of our own thoughts, feelings, and beliefs, and compassionately accept them and ourselves. From the bedrock of self-acceptance, we can nonjudgmentally and gently take inner and outer steps toward changes that promote inner peace.

By no stretch of the imagination do I always enjoy inner peace, but I have come a long way from my younger self whose thoughts and feelings often seemed to be whirling around in an emotional Cuisinart. For the most part, my older self has achieved her goal of transforming the inner Drama Queen into a Comfortable Crone who can roll with most punches and find at least a smidgen of peace and joy each day.

If I can become peaceful most of the time, I am beyond sure you can also.

All change begins with awareness. Becoming aware of what you are thinking and feeling enables you to intentionally, gently, and lovingly choose to transform attitudes and actions that are no longer working for you.

PRACTICES THAT HELP ME

- ✧ Take yourself off autopilot when first noticing turmoil and upset.
- ✧ Bring awareness to your breath. Observe your breath, as is, for a few moments. Deepen breath for a cycle or two.
- ✧ Notice your thoughts. What inner stories and statements are disturbing your peace of mind?

- ✧ Ask "Are these thoughts making me happy? Are these stories loving and constructive?"
- ✧ If the answers are "no," change the stories and thoughts to positive, self-supportive, and loving ones.

I know this process sounds simplistic, but it works. Thoughts and stories are the cornerstones feelings and attitudes rest upon. Changing them changes those. In this time of cultural upheaval, uncertainty, and divisive governing, it is incredibly easy to become resistant, angry, frightened, and overwhelmed. Simple but effective ways to keep your balance and bring peace and harmony to your assaulted soul may be just what's needed. It works for me, and I am a recovering Worry Wart and Resistance Rottweiler.

Awareness and acceptance create a climate in which inner peace can thrive.

During your day...

- ✧ Think peace. Breathe peace. Speak peace. Be peace.

> *Do not let the behavior of others*
> *disturb your inner peace.*
> —DALAI LAMA

BEING ONE WHO SEES

Women *see* a lot and are aware of even more. Our diffused and embracing energy makes us visual and emotional stimuli-sponges. We naturally scan, register, or simply notice a wide range of important and superfluous stuff. For instance, when you come home from a meeting or gathering, how many of the outfits, emotions, and stories can you remember? Probably many because it's a natural talent of ours. If you set an intention to pay attention before going, you'll remember even more. Absorbing and imprinting information and emotion, even when casually observed, make us great mothers, friends, lovers, and Jacquelines of many trades. Equally true, that same quality can wear you out. Exhaust you. Create an anxiety-ridden hag out of you. I know, because I recently exited that particular fun house.

Due to a collision of uncontrollable circumstances and over-the-top sensory stimulation, I became discouraged and overwhelmed and, as a result, descended into a mindset of awfulizing. Unfortunately, awfulizing does just that—it makes things more awful.

Luckily, I have a wise chosen-sister-friend, Juju, who helped me remember what I know. And that is, choosing to focus only on what is good for me will neutralize awfulizing and bring me back into balance and harmony. Juju said, "I focus on healing, on what's right in my awareness now, not on what is wrong with the world."

With Juju's reminder, I began to alter my focus. First, I minimized the physical discomfort as much as I could by getting noise-canceling earphones and heavy-duty earplugs. Next, I concentrated on becoming one who sees as Rumi poetically said, "Everything that is made beautiful and fair and lovely is made for the eye of one who sees." The more vividly we *see* something—whether attitude or object—the more likely we are to *get* it, both positive and negative. The Universe isn't picky about what it provides; it logically orders up whatever we obsess about. The more you see, concentrate on, think about, and visualize either woe-is-me, or yay-for-me, the more you magnetize similar energy to you.

You are the author of your awareness. As you notice, so you live.

During your day…

- ✧ Take care of physical needs.
- ✧ Sleep and rest enough. Overwhelm happens easily when you're underslept.
- ✧ Concentrate on the beautiful, fair, and lovely.

Energy flows where attention goes.
—Serge King

DANCING WITH THE DYNAMIC DUO

Awareness gives us the power to choose, and all conscious choices are valid.

Sometimes it is necessary and healing to explore difficult feelings, old wounds, and other low (interestingly, I mistyped *low* as *love* just now… hmmm) vibration feelings, thoughts, and ideas in order to move through and transform them. But the tricky part is, we can easily get mired in downer thoughts and feelings without consciously choosing to do so. Research shows our brain's natural inclination is toward negativity. As Rick Hanson, author of *Buddha's Brain*, puts it, "Your brain is like Velcro for negative experiences and Teflon for positive ones." This is where Awareness and Choice yoo-hoo at us, saying, "Come over here where the grass really *is* greener. I want to introduce you to a Dynamic Duo that will lift your hearts and make you smile."

With awareness as our guide, we can choose to dance with the dynamic duo of Amusement and Gratitude, fondly known to me as the Empress AG. Although gratitude has been my friend and companion for a long time, consciously having her team up with amusement is relatively new for me, and I find the two truly do make a dynamic difference. Given a chance, amusement loves to usurp annoyance. Being able to perceive through the eyes of amusement rather than annoyance leads to delight and indulgent adoring, the kind we feel when a beloved pet or child does something goofy or even a little naughty. Annoyance, on the other hand, typically leads to irritation and judgment, both of which can leave us circling the drain.

As a dental scaredy pants, I always ask angels to be with me at appointments. Years ago, one actually appeared. I named her Sam because she was **s**weet, **a**doring, and **m**ischievous. Only recently did I understand that the adoration I felt from her arose from amusement with and delight in me. It was a great feeling!

Amusement gives us a more loving and accepting perspective, and gratitude casts everything it touches in a more acceptable light. As Melody Beattie succinctly said, "Gratitude unlocks the fullness of life. It turns what we have into enough...." Most importantly, the qualities of amusement and gratitude help us *be enough to ourselves.*

During your day...

- ✧ Try turning annoyance into amusement.
- ✧ Give gratitude a go in a way you've never tried before.
- ✧ If you feel judgmental toward yourself, imagine yourself as a cute and appealing two-year-old doing the best she can in the moment. Allow her to enchant you.

I never lose sight of the fact that just being is fun.
—KATHARINE HEPBURN

ALIGNING WITH LOVE

Awareness generates insight.
Insight fosters understanding.
Understanding promotes love.

At the same time we are becoming stronger and owning our wisdom and power genuinely and gently, women are also empowering feminine energy to take her rightful and essential place beside masculine energy. As we create balance between the energies, it is important to remember not to demonize or dismiss either. Doing so is one reason we became so unbalanced in the first place. Both feminine and masculine energies are indispensable and noble, and, when expressing their highest nature, both are aligned with love.

To bring balance and harmony to fruition in the larger community, we are tasked with doing so within ourselves and, in so doing, create an energetic pattern others can follow. Because love strengthens, you are asked to love *yourself* into balance, harmony, and health. As you love yourself, space opens in your heart and soul, making it easier to share love with others.

Awakened by a long-awaited awareness of the importance of self-care and self-compassion, we are taking it to heart and aligning with love. By loving, understanding, and trusting ourselves more completely, we are able to connect with other women more honestly. We are not only coming to wakefulness but also coming *together*, and therein lies our major strength.

Awareness is our ally on this all-important quest. A second of awareness gives us the opportunity to question, "Whoops! Was what I just thought, said, and did aligned with love?" Awareness helps us reset our emotional, mental, and spiritual compasses in order to move more easily in the direction of love.

During your day...

- ✧ Align with your higher self and move in the direction of love.
- ✧ If only for a minute at a time, gently release notions of right and wrong, good and bad, true and false and embrace understanding and acceptance. Especially with yourself.

Tweet others as you want to be tweeted.
—Women's March poster

7

FRIENDSHIZ: THE ART OF STAYING SANE

I love my husband. He is my rock,
but my girlfriends are my sanity.
—MICHELLE OBAMA

I am in awe of women who have lived in many different places. Several friends of mine moved every two years as kids, and many other women I know have changed locations often as adults. A few even think of moving as an adventure. Amazingly, they seem sane, and I am overwhelmingly impressed by their strength and resilience. Starting at eighteen when I went out of state to college and knew absolutely no one, each of the six times I've moved to a different state I've felt like a house plant jerked out of my pot, roots flailing around wildly, or drooping morosely, with no soil or water in sight. It's the absence of in-town girlfriends that throws me for a loop, and in each move, it was a new friend who helped me regain my sanity and strength.

Women are simply wonderful, and our friendships with them play many roles: safe havens, launching pads, carnival rides, mind expanders, medications, Thelma and Louise adventures, universities of wisdom and practicality, sanitariums, and oases. I'm sure you can add a zillion more reasons why friendships are essential to you.

GUIDING INNER ELEPHANTS

Use a sweet tongue, courtesy, and tenderness, and thou
mayst manage to guide an elephant with a hair.

—SAADI

I love the preceding quote by Persian poet Saadi. Not only does the visual make me smile, but it also reminds me to be gentle with myself, to be a sweet-tongued, kind, and tender friend to Sue. Because, ideally, the nearest and dearest girlfriend we have resides within. Most of us are aware, in our heads at least, that the more loving we are to ourselves, the more loving we can be to others. It's as if those who sincerely love themselves radiate light and those who don't are more likely to cast shadows.

In our hurry-up, super-productive, 24/7 world, it's easy to feel as if responsibilities, obligations, and commitments have reached elephantine proportions. To a great extent, how good a friend you are to yourself determines whether or not you are trampled under the weight of expectations and realities or take them in stride.

Because treating yourself gently is encouraging and supportive, it gives you boosts of energy to move through your day with greater ease, strength, and grace. Treating yourself harshly depletes energy reserves and increases stress levels dramatically. Burdened by stress and sucked dry of energy, you can hardly guide an earwig, let alone an elephant.

Close your eyes for a moment and unhurriedly scan your body. If there is an area asking for your attention, notice how it feels and, with a sweet tongue, ask why it is feeling as it is. The answer may come as a thought, feeling, or actual words. The way you receive responses is uniquely yours. All ways are okay. As a dear friend would, tenderly ask how you can help.

As I did this exercise with you, I noticed my teeth were clenched and knew without asking that the reason was fear of not having enough time. Instead of using a hair to guide my inner elephants, I use a long kitty whisker donated by our cat, Riley. So, in my mind's theater, I softly ran the whisker over my jaws and reassured myself. My mind still has doubts, but my jaws are happier due to the attention and caring they received.

During your day…

- ✧ Radiate the warm light of tender friendship to yourself first.…
- ✧ Choose courtesy and kindness.
- ✧ Guide your inner elephants with a hair of choice.

INTERTWINING THREADS

Optimally, friendships include an equal exchange of energy between participants. Great friendships involve times of giving and times of receiving. Although friendship has many aspects, three essential qualities I'd like to share are

- ✧ **Loyalty**: Because I'm an Aries, loyalty is a must for me. I cherish friends who can be counted on to be in my corner no matter what the situation. Not that they will agree with me, particularly, but that I know they have my back. I see loyalty as a commitment to support and be there for a friend or loved one.
- ✧ **Love**: Love may be too all-encompassing a word. Some friendships are held together by feelings less loaded, such as genuinely liking and enjoying another's company and personality. Whether you love, like, or

love *and* like particular friends, it's fundamental to wish them well no matter what and support them to the best of your ability.

✧ **Laughter**: Most friendships enjoy the magical elixir of laughter. And it's a good thing, because friendships have ups and downs, as do individuals within them, and sometimes laughter is about the only thing that can elevate our attitudes and lighten our hearts.

While intimate friendships are indispensable, life-enhancing, and sanity-protecting, casual friendships also widen our circles of connection and fill our hearts with joy. One of my Dove candy wrappers shared this wise tidbit: "Friendship is the gold thread that ties hearts together." I firmly believe the experiences we share, depth of understanding between us, lessons we learn, tears we shed, and wisdom we gather with each other's help create a web of intertwining golden threads that connect all of our hearts. We are held in the embrace of our personal friendships and, collectively, bask in the grace of all other friendships as well.

During your day…

✧ Honor friends who have sustained you over the years by letting them know how important they were/ are to you.

✧ Create an altar to friendship.

✧ Reminisce about a few favorite laughs or crying jags with friends.

Friends have your back and hug your front.

LISTENING, A GIFT OF PRESENCE

Our minds love to provide answers. Puzzles, our own problems, others' dilemmas, world peace. You name it, and we either think we have an answer or wish we did. One of the best ways to love friends is to ignore the deluge of answers flooding your mind as they share what's on theirs. Just listen. Most of us long to be *heard*. In our frenetic society, it is almost a miracle to have people *pay attention* to you without glancing at their phone or cutting you short with suggestions.

I believe the most reliable answers are found within our own hearts and minds and, because I am a verbal processer, talking usually helps me plow around inside for solutions. When someone really listens to me—or I truly listen to myself—words act like little shovels removing inner debris and letting me see more clearly. My shovels have been busy recently resolving a relationship issue I've struggled with for years. Although a smaller version of the issue will probably always exist, it no longer bothers me.

Many people loved and listened to me along the way, but I finally turned a healing corner with the help of a new friend. As well as being a superlative listener, my friend Lea is an experienced grief counselor. During several get-togethers, Lea's intense and interested attention—punctuated by occasional clarifying questions—encouraged me to dive deeply into grief I'd been avoiding and, many tears later, accept the reality that any change in the situation would undoubtedly be mine. Lea's gift of presence helped me free myself from resistance and longing, allowed me to tap into snoozing strength and wisdom, and take full responsibility for my own happiness. Not surprisingly, life has become immeasurably sunnier.

Because I had asked for help and Lea sees our relationship as reciprocal, I believe there was definitely divine orchestration at work in our meeting.

During your day...

- ✧ Truly and deeply listen to yourself. Ask yourself a question, if one pops into your mind. Or just say "Hi" and listen for a few minutes.
- ✧ If the opportunity presents itself, be absolutely present—with no agenda—to a friend or loved one for five minutes. Notice how it feels.

The feminine quality of presence is
one of the most precious gifts we can give.

STUMBLING, GRUMBLING, GROWING, GRIEVING...

We all need safe people with whom we can kibitz about life, who hold our hands and hearts as we stumble, grumble, grow, and grieve. If you were fortunate, your mother—and maybe father—probably filled some of those needs, at least when you were young.

Just for fun, let's walk down Memory Lane for a few minutes to enjoy glimpses of gratitude toward those who were your cohorts, guides, and gurus during the childhood and teen seasons of your life. Who did you giggle with over getting your first bra? Who gave you tips on making out, or like me, did you stumble through that milestone on your own? Who helped you grow and learn to make good decisions? Who did you go to, hold on to, and grieve with when your heart was breaking? Who could you count on to protect you? Who gave you "the talk" if there was one?

Did you like yourself, and were you able to be a safe person to yourself then?

Moving forward through young adulthood and midlife, who are your go-to people for learning about falling in love, being dumped, making commitments, being a mother or deciding not to be? Who guides you though the evolution that comes when taking on responsibility for yourself and, possibly, a family? What and who help you navigate work? To whom can you turn for solace as those you love and count on die, your kids leave the nest, and your body feels its limitations? Still vibrant but with fewer responsibilities, who helps mid-wife you into ever greater authenticity and emotional freedom? If you are as chronologically gifted as I am, what mainstays are in place for you? Who are you playing with? What soul-soaring activities do you take part in?

Who helps you remember your innate strength and inspires you to call up courage and fortitude you didn't know you had? Who takes care of you if you need it?

Who are your partners-in-eldering, those who freely and joyously drink from the fountain of accrued wisdom with you? Who will lovingly be with you as you cross the ultimate threshold?

Do you like yourself, and are you able to be a safe person with yourself now?

During your day…

- ✧ Remember those who have helped you find your strength throughout your life. Reach out to them with a visit, call, email, text, or prayer of thanks.
- ✧ Remember those for whom you were, or are, present in important and strengthening ways and give yourself a hug of appreciation.
- ✧ Lovingly be a safe shelter for yourself as you stumble, grumble, grow, and grieve.

The woman's soul is fashioned as a shelter
in which other souls may unfold.
—EDITH STEIN

WASHING WINDOWS

Friends "do windows." When we have lost confidence, friends can wash the windows of our psyches that have been obscured. I've found that friends aren't always flesh and blood, or may have been at one time but have left their body for greener heavenly pastures.

A couple of years ago, I was preparing to lead a weekend retreat for forty women from my church. I'd had a great time throughout the year planning the content and was excited about doing it. That is, I was excited until, for reasons I still don't fully understand, one of my dearest friends—a person whom I'd been close to for twenty-five years—stopped calling and often didn't answer my calls. She denied anything was wrong but continued to be unavailable and unresponsive. Since rejection has always been a hot button for me, I was devastated. My heart cracked open, and my previous retreat confidence and excitement seeped out while I grieved a loss I neither understood nor could control.

Flesh-and-blood women like my daughter-in-love, Colleen, washed the windows of my soul by listening, encouraging, and pointing out my strengths. Their cheerleading really helped, but I was still nowhere near optimum-retreat-leader capacity. In response to my increasingly desperate prayers, three angelically orchestrated window washings happened. First, I had a touching dream in which the main character was honored for leading several people to safety in a disaster zone. Since all aspects of our dreams usually represent us, I took that as an affirmation and an attagirl from my subconscious. Second, a day or so after that dream, I was going through some old paperwork and ran across the copy of a seven-year-old email from another chosen daughter in which she outlined why she loved our relationship and me. Wow, what a wonderful "coincidence." And third, no more than an hour later, I found a several-year-old thank-you note from a dear friend whose hand I had been holding when she died two years before. A very, very sweet and uplifting note. Okay, I'm tearing up now as I write and was downright bawling then.

Thanks to in-the-flesh friends and angelic assistance—both before and during—the retreat was a high point of my life. And, after a few weeks' hiatus, my longtime friend slowly returned.

During your day...

✧ If you are having a hard time seeing your worth and lovability, let friends—incarnate and other-worldly—wash your soul's windows for you.

> *There is no better looking glass than an old friend.*
> —HINDU PROVERB

BEING COMMUNITY

When my spiritual mother, Annabelle, welcomed me into her heart with the phrase "You were born of my heart, our bloodline is spirit," she was *being* community. Each time you open your heart to someone else, you are *being* community. Each time you applaud another's success, listen to a friend as she struggles through loss, babysit so a mom can have some quiet time, or take food to a grieving family, you are personifying community. Ideally, our communities shelter, sustain, nurture, challenge, forgive, celebrate, have fun, connect, value, and *see* us, and we do the same for others involved.

I bet you are gifted at being a valuable member *in* communities of all types and that you excel at *providing* community for family, friends, colleagues, causes, total strangers, and probably four-legged critters as well. And now the trick question: How skilled are you at *being* community for yourself? If you can answer yes to the following statements, good for you! You are great at being community for yourself.

- ✧ I usually speak to myself as I would to a good friend.
- ✧ I can count on myself for forgiveness.
- ✧ I take care of my physical, emotional, mental, and spiritual wants and needs.
- ✧ I enjoy my own company.
- ✧ I believe in my goodness, strength, and worthiness.
- ✧ I love myself.

If some of your answers are no, please don't be discouraged. Being a loving community for ourselves can be a lifelong endeavor. When I first met Annabelle, I was a quivering mass of vulnerability plastered over with fear and rage, barely able to provide a stable community for my two little boys, let alone be anything except a hateful judge for myself. Annabelle encouraged and challenged me to embark on the journey of loving and forgiving myself and, as a result, I am often able to create a safe internal community for Sue. As Annabelle's favorite poster—Ziggy, shaking his fist at God saying, "It ain't easy being human, ya know!"— underscored, being your own safe haven is a process. Often not an easy one. Like many of us are, I'm still working at it.

During your day (life)...

◇ Become a safe, sheltering, encouraging community for yourself and your numerous subpersonalities.

◇ Find a loving, encouraging, and wise Annabelle when you need one.

It ain't easy being human, ya know!
—Ziggy

But you can do it!
—Sue

BEATING YOUR BREAST

Some women are internal processers and work through emotions in solitude. Others of us are more emotive and need to express feelings outwardly in order to process them fully and successfully. I process as I talk; my thoughts become more cohesive when I hear them out loud or write them by hand. Most of us process both ways. During times of high stress, anguish, or frustration, you may need to metaphorically beat your breast. To emerge from particularly dense emotional jungles, external processers need to physically expel excess energy by stalking around, Tarzan style, and get it out—preferably with a bitch-buddy who can witness and support you emotionally.

On the night I found out my first husband was in love/lust with a woman I had erroneously considered a good friend, I don't know what would have happened without my bitch-buddy, Nan. After the revelation, I escaped to Nan's house. Unable to sleep, Nan and I—with a little help from Napa Valley—laughed and sobbed our way through increasingly outlandish and hilarious revenge scenarios. Because of Nan's loving presence, and our ability to play and rage together, I released enough trauma-energy to go home the next morning without murder on my mind. Well, not at the *forefront* of my mind at least...

When needed, bitch-buddies help us stay sane. Also, because they see us at our most raw, naked, and vulnerable, bitch-buddies *must* be completely trustworthy. And vice versa.

Take a moment to muse about how you process feelings. All ways are okay as long as they represent who you authentically are. If you process quietly and alone because as a child you knew it was best to shut up and be unobtrusive, ponder other ways that might work for you. If your genuine expressive mode is external, do you have a friend—or special bitch-buddy—with whom to emote? If you avoid processing by ignoring or denying emotion, is that working for you?

Deep listening is miraculous for both listener and speaker. When someone receives us with open-hearted, nonjudging, intensely interested listening, our spirits expand.

During your day...

- ✧ Notice your feelings with love and allowing.
- ✧ Share your sacred, tender emotions only in safe places with safe people.
- ✧ Be an amused and adoring bitch-buddy for yourself.

*A true friend acts as a confessional for purging
grief and a kiln in which to fire strength.*

GATHERING TO YOUR HEART

Compassionate friends are capable of, and willing to, gather us to their hearts with empathy. They willingly feel our pain *with* us, not in a codependent, I-need-to-fix-you way, but in an *I-see-you-and-I-understand* way.

My friend Clarice shared this beautiful story of being gathered to someone's heart:

> I had dragged myself to the Friday evening portion of a women's weekend retreat right after finding out my son was drinking again. No one knew my heart was broken, but during an exercise in which we were to walk around the room connecting with others by making eye contact and touching, the second person I looked at *saw* my pain. Without a word, she sensed where I was—sad, helpless, grieving, and guilty—and simply held me. Other retreatants continued the exercise around us, but she never let me go. I was holding it all together until she cradled my head in her hand. It might as well have been my heart, for that tender touch brought out all the tears concerning my son's addiction that I'd stored for twenty years. We stood there, both crying, our tummies bouncing against each other, as she silently shared my heartbreak. Those few minutes were so nurturing and healing that I still tear up every time I remember them.

Clarice's experience is an example of feminine energy at its finest; the ability to sense another's pain and share the energy in compassionate, noninvasive, healing ways. This kind of sharing is not jumping in a hole of suffering with another; rather, it is the art of creating a container of love in which pain is allowed to be experienced and can then transform. Shared energy strengthens both the person experiencing it and those privileged to bear witness.

During your day...

⬧ Celebrate the feminine strength and sensitivity that is your birthright.

> *Attention without feeling, I began to learn, is*
> *only a report. An openness—an empathy—was*
> *necessary if the attention was to matter.*
>
> —MARY OLIVER

ALLOWING OTHERS TO HELP

A friend of mind had rotator cuff surgery this week, and although she wasn't nervous about the surgery itself, she was very apprehensive about lining up the help she and her dog would need during her weeks of recovery. At our presurgery lunch, she said, "I'm not very good at this asking for help stuff." Have you ever said that? I sure have. And I've heard the same admission from countless others. It seems many of us are uncomfortable accepting advocacy or help of any kind. It's often easier to accept assistance when we pay for it or when we're sure we can reciprocate in kind.

Isn't it strange that, although it feels so good to be of service to someone else, we feel so uncomfortable allowing others to do the same for us? Our hesitation probably stems, at least in part, from the desire not to be a burden exacerbated by a more deeply primal awareness of how dangerous vulnerability can be. That said, in reality, we all need help and advocacy on occasion. Advocacy can run the gamut from empathetic listening to metaphorically ripping down hospital doors and confronting difficult doctors. We need help and advocacy when we're ill, enervated, out of sorts, on our last frayed nerve, grieving, incapacitated, out of our league in terms of technology, and myriad other things. When we find ourselves in a fish-out-of-water situation flopping helplessly on a rough shore, we need to allow others to help us back to the water.

It's easier to receive help and support when you accept the fact that everyone occasionally needs advocates. Next time you need one, try changing your perspective, if need be, and making the life-affirming, and possibly life-saving, decision to willingly and graciously give others the gift of helping you. I think you'll find appreciation and gratitude are always welcome repayments.

During your day…

- ✧ Imagine yourself allowing others to help you and notice how you feel about doing so.
- ✧ Remember a time when you helped someone else and notice how that felt.

*Both givers and receivers can be blessed
by their exchange.*

WAGGING

If you have a dog, or have ever had a dog, how did you feel when it greeted you? Pretty special, right? Whether we've been gone for an hour, a day, or a week, Lily, our almost-ten-pound Maltipeekapoo, greets us as if she thought we'd never return. She's excited and joyous and waggy, and we laughingly act like ninnies returning her greeting. Do we greet anyone else with the same enthusiasm? Nope, not even close, and it would look pretty weird if we did. However, it might really help friends and family know how we felt about them if we adopted a human variation of tail wagging. In reality, HTW (human tail wagging) could actually make us feel more deeply about each other and maybe ourselves as well. Enthusiasm magnifies and enhances, and what relationship wouldn't enjoy a little enhancement?

I've read that Maya Angelou believed we are unconsciously asking each other four relationship questions all the time:

1. Do you see me?
2. Do you care that I'm here?
3. Am I enough for you, or do you need me to be better in some way?
4. Can I tell I'm special to you by the way you look at me?

Dogs almost always give a resounding "Yes!" to all four questions. Although they can't tell you they love you with words, they sure let you know via their enthusiasm and palpable joy at your presence. Dogs also seem to know when you need extra encouragement and cuddle up next to you, put their heads on your leg or foot, bug you until you get off the couch and out for a walk, simply gaze at you with adoration, or do something silly or ornery that makes you laugh.

Dogs are love gurus, so let's try an HTW experiment. When you are interacting with a friend or loved one, put down your device (dogs have a paw up in the wagging department because they don't do devices) and ask, "What would doggie do?" And then have fun bestowing a little human tail wagging.

During your day...

✧ Love first, wag often.
✧ Show enthusiasm for and with others... and yourself.

> *Do unto others as I would do unto them*
> *because it's no coincidence that the reverse of*
> *my species name is pretty high-powered.*
>
> —DOG

8

BEFRIENDING YOUR AUTHENTIC SELVES

It is not your job to like me—it is mine.
—Byron Katie

In an email recently, I was commenting on Ram Dass's iconic book *Be Here Now* and mistyped it *Be Her Now*. I like it! Let's do it. One of the best ways to Be You Now is to befriend all aspects of your multifaceted self. I discussed the concept of inner selves, which I call subpersonalities, in the meditation entitled "Reclaiming Your Selves" in chapter 1. I will be talking about our many-dimensional selves again throughout this chapter.

As the saying goes, there is strength in diversity, and within you are many different personality traits, individual characteristics, and special talents that combine to make you a wise, empowered woman. Strength is increased exponentially when all aspects of ourselves accept each other and play well together in the inner tribe of our being. Ill-will toward denied or shunned parts of your self undermines your self-confidence and tears at the underpinnings of your strength, which is why it's important to heal and transform subpersonalities by giving them the love and attention they need.

The key to inner strength is self-acceptance and self-compassion. Life hums along more happily when you have your back, hug your front, and delight in all aspects of your being. When your quirky, clever, and amazingly diversified inner individuals coalesce to shape unique and authentic you, they create a citadel of inner balance and harmony. The best strength training you can do is knowing and embracing your inner selves.

Authenticity is attainable; perfection is not. Authenticity is a beacon of light, a touchstone of realness in a world awash in falsehoods and fabrication. While perfectionism places us in a never-good-enough prison, authenticity liberates us.

RETIRING THE CHAMELEON

Early in life we become skilled at sensing the atmosphere around us and learn to choose actions, attitudes, and subpersonalities appropriate to the situation. Those are healthy choices designed to ensure safety and promote happiness. If, however, we feel unsafe, are addicted to approval, or feel overly responsible for the moods of others, we can become a habitual chameleon, changing affect, attitude, and personalities in order to protect ourselves and appease others.

For instance, if you are raised in an alcoholic, abusive, or anger-fueled family, it's natural to become adept at being whomever you think might calm the situation. Many adult children of alcoholics I've worked with admit to trying to be as invisible as possible. Janice, my client, said: "When Dad was drinking, I just tried to get as small as possible in order not to draw his attention. I have kind of a large personality, like my mom, but, over the years, both of us sort of got smaller and smaller until we didn't even talk when he was home."

Janice's situation was dramatic, and she and her mom possibly made a life-saving decision to become invisible. In therapy, Janice was hoping to retire her chameleon self-protective persona and become the outgoing person she authentically was. Many of us have more subtle motivations for changing our natural colors in order to please, avert confrontation, make things run more smoothly, etc. I'm sure you can add your own reasons here.

There are also more subtle reasons for becoming a chameleon. Trudy, a sensitive and artistic child, was born into a family of competitive athletes. She tried to like and succeed in sports but, having neither the desire nor talent to do so, felt like an outsider. To assuage her fear of not belonging, as an adult, Trudy became whomever she thought would be acceptable to whatever group she happened to be with at the time. Her goal in therapy was to embrace and accept herself completely in order to fully belong to *herself* no matter where she was or what she was doing. Although challenging, that loving quality of self-care is life affirming and life changing.

We have many genuine inner personalities in our repertoire, and expressing them enhances authenticity. On the other hand, assuming a false self in order to please others and/or fit in is outer-directed and plays havoc with self-confidence and authenticity.

During your day...

- ✧ Be a compassionate and understanding observer of your actions and attitudes.
- ✧ Gently be aware of any chameleon temptations. With great kindness, ask yourself what your motivation is— fear, desire for acceptance, the urge to avoid conflict? What do you need from yourself right now to make those catalysts less compelling?
- ✧ With awareness, choose authenticity whenever appropriate and safe. In many complex situations, becoming a Compassionate Observer may be the healthiest choice.

When you are your authentic self, you have no competition.
—Anonymous

LIVING IN RESONANCE

Remember what it feels like when you know you've made the wrong decision but there is no going back? I might use the word *heartsick* to describe such a feeling. Each time we act in ways that don't resonate with our hearts, we cause a little heartsickness, a sense of disharmony in the very essence of our beings. Our physical hearts are not only the drumbeat of our physical beingness but also home to our moral compass and innate goodness. Therefore, life flows more freely and happily when you are living in resonance with your heart's harmony.

Because our hearts naturally, and of necessity, go *out* to others, it is easy to forget how essential it is for our hearts to go *in* to ourselves. However, it is crucial you also act *out* on your own behalf with mindful and compassionate attention.

To be truly authentic, we each need to listen, and dance to, the distinctive tune our heart is humming.

Authenticity is absolutely individual. Yet, how often do we forgo what our hearts resonate with in order to fit in, be liked, not rock the boat, and take the seemingly easy way out. Not listening to the song of your heart is usually the result of fear. Ignoring your heart song and, therefore, feeling out of resonance with yourself can be as small as ordering the "wrong" thing at a restaurant. But it can also be as wounding as speaking without first engaging your heart's wisdom and creating a fissure in a relationship. Or as life altering as choosing a career or mate based on what others expect or want from you. A client once said, "Walking down the aisle toward the altar, I looked at my husband-to-be and thought 'This is a mistake!'" Not listening to her heart's authentic—albeit a bit tardy—warning, Elaine spent the next twelve years trying to convince herself she'd made the right choice. "Although the eventual divorce was hurtful, it *saved my life... at least my heart*," Elaine said.

Living in resonance with the dreams and ideals of your unique heart is a surefire way to strengthen authenticity.

During your day...

✦ Check in with your heart. A simple moment of attention, a silent question—Is this a good idea? What feels right and loving here?—is usually all it takes to know.

✦ Every now and then, notice if your heart is humming contentedly or if it feels discordant. Depending on the quality of humming, follow up. Ask who or what might benefit from mindful attention.

✦ Honor your heart's powerful wisdom.

*True strength has the courage to
outwardly express inner authenticity.*

RECOGNIZING EMOTIONAL HIGH MAINTENANCE

As mentioned in the meditation "Getting to Know Me" in chapter 3, I've known I was a highly sensitive person (HSP) for many years. A few years ago, after moving through a tough emotional period, I made up an additional diagnosis for myself, that of being emotionally high maintenance. The most sobering awareness was how much I wanted others to do the maintenance for me. I'm referring to emotional maintenance. Everyday small stuff like comments that cause me to question myself or chilly attitudes from others that make me wonder if I've done something wrong. Everyday happenings I take personally and cause me to judge myself—or others—harshly.

Similar to being an HSP, being an emotionally high maintenance person (EHMP) is a gift with an edge. It usually means you are highly sensitive to others' feelings, as well as your own, and quick to offer kindness, compassion, and empathy. You are usually a wonderful friend and helpful to those in need. The edge is you feel things deeply and can easily become hurt, defensive, irritated, depressed, and anxious.

If you are resonating with EHM-ness, you've probably been called *over*sensitive, which can easily lead to believing there is something wrong with you. It took me a long time to believe I wasn't faulty and was wired to be highly sensitive from conception.

The gift of sensitivity is easier to live with when you learn how to take the edge off. The best way I've found to soften my resistance is to follow this blueprint:

- ✧ **Aware**: Recognize your sensitive nature and loving heart and know that vulnerability and mindful maintenance are part of the package.
- ✧ **Acknowledge**: Know your gift is precious and requires gentle care and tender understanding in order to maintain your emotional well-being.
- ✧ **Allow**: Invite a higher view by stepping back and dispassionately observing what is while refraining from judging or overdramatizing.
- ✧ **Accept**: Honor the reality that your sensitive nature will need life-long recognition and maintenance, and you are the major source of both.
- ✧ **Embrace**: Arrival at this stage allows us to appreciate lessons learned, growth achieved, and silver linings as a result of our sensitivity.

Awareness helps you find ways to care for yourself. What fuel works best for you? How do you know you're running on empty? What oils your soul and keeps your life running smoothly? Do whatever strengthens your ability to cope with and enjoy life.

SOME THINGS THAT WORK FOR ME

- ✧ Talk with trusted people to expel energy and sort feelings, not to get "fixed."
- ✧ Find the subpersonality who is hurting and become a good mother to her.
- ✧ Call on and hang out with my Spiritual Crew, both human and angelic.
- ✧ Go to therapy when needed.
- ✧ Pause… wait… breathe…. When in need of emotional maintenance, it's easy to say and do things we regret and that, of course, makes things worse.
- ✧ Spend quiet time alone.

During your day…

- ✧ Recognize when you are hurting, drained, or tired and lovingly take care of yourself.
- ✧ Change self-chastisement energy to supportive and soothing actions and words.
- ✧ Make appropriate amends to self and others.

Accepting who you are now gives you an ever deepening awareness of who you are becoming.

EMBRACING FOIBLES AND VULNERABILITIES

Our heads know that befriending and supporting our many authentic selves help us become stronger and better able to confront the external vicissitudes of life; however, our training, hearts, and guts are continuously judging us for real and imagined faults and weaknesses. In reality, everyone has foibles and vulnerabilities. Given the right attitude, they can provide the building blocks for many strengths. Empathy, for example, often arises from an understanding of our own vulnerable underbellies. Befriending yourself fills internal energy tanks and augments your life force, whereas judgment, nonsupportive attitudes, and disparaging self-talk blast a hole in your energy reservoir.

Contrary to the "no pain, no gain" philosophy, understanding and embracing are the most effective ways to help ourselves change. Understanding, acceptance, and empathy are transformative. Judgment and chastisement rarely create long-term, sustainable change. For most of us, nonjudgmentally embracing our foibles and vulnerabilities is a life-long, onion-peeling adventure. Because of the ceaseless nature of self-acceptance, patience is required.

I consistently return to the following threefold process to help me accept my own and also others' foibles and vulnerabilities with the intention of transforming judgment into embracing.

WHEN DISCOMFORT OR JUDGMENT ARISE

1. *Take responsibility* for my feelings. No matter what happens, how I *feel* about it is my responsibility. Feelings arise out of our own minds and experiences. When we forget to take responsibility, it's easy to project blame onto others.
2. *Neutralize judgment* with acknowledgment and acceptance. I keep it simple by saying, "Ah, so, here I am judging. Okay." Of course, acceptance is easier when I can acknowledge judgment with humor or amusement.
3. *Feel the feeling*, the bedrock/underlying/primal feeling that is usually based in fear. When acknowledged and accepted, the energy of most feelings will begin to transform.

Even though it's often a life-long learning curve, the legacy of being aware of and embracing all aspects of yourself is increased wisdom, joy, self-love, and freedom.

During your day...

✧ Become increasingly aware of your feelings.

◈ Be curious and entertained by your feelings and foibles rather than judgmental.

◈ Know that self-acceptance becomes easier with practice... and chuckles.

Have patience. All things are difficult before they become easy.
—Saadi

BEARING THE TORCH

Women are torchbearers. If you are struggling in the dark with a relationship, emotional growth spurt, or mothering questions, for instance, a sister or friend can light that darkness with her wisdom and empathy. When grief is acute and the darkness impenetrable, your understanding and accepting presence acts as a lightening agent.

A natural strength for most women is the ability and willingness to share honestly and supportively. Feelings, wisdom, recipes, experiences, compassion are all fodder for helping each other grow and evolve. The Buddha reportedly said, "When words are both true and kind, they can change our world." The wise, empathetic, empowered aspects of our selves excel at sharing kind and true words at just the right time. And, if no words are appropriate or helpful, loving silence easily bears the light of kindness and caring.

As torchbearers and way-showers, we lead and inspire others toward their dreams and aspirations. But, as always, your first and most important calling is to light your own soul's path. As you authentically explore, heal, and grow in self-love and compassion, your light naturally burns brighter, helping to brighten and uplift everything around you.

Annabelle, my spiritual mother, began calling me a torchbearer while I was still neck deep in fear, loathing, and resentment. At the time, it made me mad. And scared me. What?! I could barely drag myself out of bed in the morning to feed the kids and get them off to school before dissolving in tears or beating the !%*#! out of a punching bag. At best, any torch I had was smoldering and polluting the atmosphere with sooty smoke. Because of that and the fact I'd been thoroughly indoctrinated not to "toot my own horn" or "get a big head," even the possibility of *having* a torch was beyond belief. But Annabelle had planted a seed…

You are a torchbearer.

Thankfully, the only responsibility connected to accepting "You are a torchbearer" is being true to yourself and intending that light will flow from all aspects of your being.

During your day…

⬧ Allow the idea of being a torchbearer to permeate your mind. Have fun musing about how you can (and undoubtedly already do) effortlessly bear and share more light in your life and world.

✧ Please remember to tend to your own torch first in order to keep its light strong and steady.

As we let our own light shine, we unconsciously give other people permission to do the same. As we are liberated from our fear, our presence automatically liberates others.
—MARIANNE WILLIAMSON

FREEING MAMA BEAR

The mama bear I encourage you to free is a mature, wise, and protective instinct within you. She is willing to rise up on her hind legs and do what it takes to keep you safe, healthy, and treated respectfully. Her intent is never to defeat or maim others but simply to look out for your well-being—and often the well-being of others. An astute and evolved mama bear is committed to helping you honor reasonable, inner-directed limits and boundaries. She also keeps you from accepting *un*acceptable behaviors and situations, those emanating *from* you and those directed *toward* you.

One of the best ways mama bears help us is to lovingly but firmly rein in the unhealed aspects of ourselves who tend to *fight*, *flee*, or *freeze* when feeling threatened and/or angry. Anger can be either *de*structive or *con*structive. Destructive anger is ignited by fear and lashes out in attacking, relationship-shattering ways designed to avoid and deny underlying feelings of hurt and helplessness. Being both cruel and blaming, destructive anger is the antithesis of feminine energy. On the other hand, a mature mama bear's constructive anger is aware, calm, and often empathetic toward the people or circumstances causing it. Constructive anger makes win-win choices. It consults, listens, and, when necessary, insists… consistently. Constructive, feminine anger is committed to positive change and better understanding. Such constructive confrontation can often build bridges of cooperation between dissimilar people.

Does knowing that constructive anger is the only kind that works mean it's the only kind you'll experience from now on? Nope. But it *can* become the only kind you choose to *act from*.

During your day…

- ✧ Become aware of difficult feelings, especially anger. Without judgment or shame, offer love and acceptance to yourself as you experience tough feelings.
- ✧ Acknowledge and honor your feelings in ways that speak to your heart. I might name a feeling and ask, "Who within me is feeling this shame? What is the origin of this feeling?" Invite your self-compassionate mama bear to help you gently explore the feelings.
- ✧ Cool off. It's usually a good idea *not* to act from your flash point, whether you flash into flames or flash-

freeze. Cooling off periods can last minutes or months depending on the circumstances.

✧ Choose to act in powerful, productive ways you can be proud of. It's often necessary to muse and heal before knowing how to respond. Although waiting to clear things up is not easy, doing so gives you a better chance of speaking and acting authentically.

*Say what you **mean**. **Mean** what you say.*
*Don't be **mean** when you say it.*
—MERYL RUNION

UNVEILING ESSENCE

Each of us is essentially Spirit wrapped in a miraculous human body. I believe we choose to incarnate in order to hone our souls in ways only available in the dense energy of flesh. I also feel the divine aspect of self remembers its eternal identity and, consequently, is lighthearted, unfailingly wise, continually peaceful, and permanently filled with loving-kindness. The challenging thing is, our spiritual essence—the most effortless and authentic aspect of our being—is illusive. Most of us, including those sincerely engaged in spiritual practice, effectively shroud our essence with everyday uncertainty, negative thoughts, striving, activities, and other diversions.

Why is that?

Several reasons spring to mind. For starters, life is incredibly compelling and distracting. Plus, it is far easier to respond to the loudest shouts and most raucous demands and expectations than it is to pay attention to the soft, ethereal echoes of our souls. At least for me, another reason is the tendency to doubt. Having been told in countless ways that "we're only human," our earthbound selves doubt whether we're worthy of claiming spiritual heritage, wonder if it's all a bunch of pie-in-the-sky wishful thinking anyway, and are pretty sure *we* can't tune into essence, God, Spirit, or whatever we call Source.

Let's pretend disbelief and doubt have been dispelled for the time being. Pick a time and cozy place where you won't be interrupted and allow your eyes to close. Gently move your awareness through your body thanking it for being your dependable means for experiencing physical life. Appreciate your body. Now, effortlessly bring attention to your heart area and imagine your breath inhaling and exhaling through it. In front of you, visualize a beautiful diaphanous veil slightly swaying to the rhythm of your breath. Behind the veil, a soothingly soft light is emanating from your spiritual essence who is patiently and affectionately loving you. She literally has all the time in—and out of—the world, so no hurry or effort is required. Relax in her presence. Just *be* for a few moments. Notice what you are sensing and feeling. Rest and relax, soaking in the essence of the experience. Gently bring your attention back to your heart and thank it, and your imagination, for giving you the gift of this meditation… whatever it was or wasn't.

During your day…

✧ Rest and delight in the presence of your Spiritual Essence. Use the preceding meditation or invite your intuition and imagination to show you another way.

Nothing can dim the light that shines from within.
—MAYA ANGELOU

BEFRIENDING MORTALITY

Even though death is a common denominator among every living being, we often struggle to befriend the reality. We know we will die but subconsciously don't really *believe* it. At least that was my experience until I was compelled to make a concerted effort to make friends with mortality.

In my late twenties I was told by a respected teacher that I needed to befriend death before I could really live. Because I was an insecure, terrified, about-to-be single mom, his admonition sailed right over my head. A few years later, my soul dredged up that long-buried comment, and I became obsessed with reading everything I could about the subject. Reading led me to workshops with death and dying pioneer Dr. Elisabeth Kübler-Ross and eventually into hospice work.

About ten years after my obsession with death began, my wonderful mother was diagnosed with terminal cancer. Because of the work and self-reflection I'd done, I was truly able to *be* with Mother throughout her final journey. Being with Mother in those eighteen months was challenging and profound, terrifying and rewarding, exhausting and exhilarating, and incredibly meaningful for us both. There was definitely some angelic intervention around my compulsion to study and befriend death, I believe.

Befriending mortality doesn't mean numbing yourself to the feelings surrounding death, loss, and grief. Because we are emotional beings, of course, we grieve losses and rail against the pain, anxiety, and sorrow that can be a part of the dying process. If you have come to grips with mortality, catharsis is a healing way for your compassionate heart to release and transform pent-up energy. On the other hand, if you express from a resistant or victimized position, catharsis often becomes a self-sabotaging loop.

Naturally, you will befriend mortality differently than I did. But, please, if you haven't already, I urge you to gently, respectfully, and compassionately face any fears or beliefs you have about death that prevent you from making peace with the reality. Befriending mortality is one of the most freeing and strength-producing things you can do for yourself.

During your day…

- ✧ Entertain the idea of death, being mindful of your feelings as you do.
- ✧ On paper, with a trusted friend, or in the safety of your heart, have a conversation about your end-of-life beliefs.
- ✧ If death is anathema to you, take gentle baby steps as you explore.

> *Death is more universal than life;*
> *everyone dies but not everyone lives.*
> —ANDREW SACHS

ENFOLDING IN KINDNESS

As touched on in the previous meditation, we are sparks of the Divine, offspring of the Beloved, and reflections of Love. Our core self is whole and holy. Because we are visiting Earth right now, seemingly far from our spiritual home, it's not unusual to feel vaguely unmoored. While it's wonderful to know we are both human and divine, it can also be discombobulating to both aspects of our being. As you go about your jam-packed life learning human lessons and having a great time in this decidedly sensory playground, you may notice inklings of loneliness for... for what?

Dr. Elisabeth Kübler-Ross, psychiatrist and noted teacher on death and dying, taught that human illnesses can symbolize a soul's homesickness for Home. I found out the hard way that some children, disenchanted by human life and so homesick for the spiritual realm, sicken and die. At age seven, my vibrant son Brett became so ill he lost a third of his body weight. Doctors could find nothing wrong with him. Frantic, I asked Annabelle, the intuitive counselor who would become my spiritual mother, to tune into him. Annabelle found that his soul, knowing it was time to begin forgetting his previous spiritual connections and fully engage with earthly life, was resisting spiritual amnesia and struggling with the choice to stay or leave. From an early age, Brett had seen angels and played on clouds with Jesus while he slept; consequently, Annabelle's discovery didn't surprise me.

Thankfully, he stayed, forgot, and fully immersed himself in the physical realm. Not surprisingly, now in midlife, Brett is re-remembering and deeply invested in spiritual study and practice.

While our human self may have forgotten spirit-existence, our transcendent self never does. I trust some of the indescribable feelings I face are symbols of spiritual homesickness. Maybe yours are too. One of the best ways to befriend both the celestial and corporeal aspects of your being is to unfailingly enfold yourself in kindness.

Wrapped in a cocoon of kindness, both our human and holy selves can savor joy and growth more completely and remain consistently strong and courageous throughout life's challenges.

During your day...

- ✧ Create kindness corners in your heart and home; a portable safe haven as well as an at-home sanctuary metaphorically affirming Kindness Lives Here.
- ✧ Enfold your Selves in kindness, a quality both mortal and divine.

> *Be kinder to yourself. And then let your*
> *kindness flood the world.*
> —PEMA CHÖDRÖN

9

ALLOWING WHAT IS

Just allow. Allow in love. Allow pain. Allow desire.
Allow learning. Allow healing. Allow frustration.
Allow uncertainty. Allow yourself to experience what
you must experience and learn what you need to learn,
so that your uniqueness can emerge organically.

—Vironika Tugaleva

In my quest for peace of mind and the strength it promotes, the need to accept unwanted circumstances loomed large. During the often arduous journey, I found *allowing* to be a necessary step before I could get all the way to acceptance. In fact, it turned out acceptance was a major hurdle on my trek toward less resentment and a calmer, happier me. Well, maybe it was actually *resistance* to acceptance that was the stumbling block. Nonetheless, I needed a bridge from the troubled waters of resistance and anger to the calmer shores of acceptance and embracing and found it in *allowing*.

This chapter was initially named "Accepting What Is," but thinking some of you might have run into the same resistance I did, I chose to use *allowing* as the first step in our aim of increased inner peace, receptive wisdom, and courageous power.

> *Allow:* Neutralize resistance by dispassionately observing and distancing yourself from the drama in situations and relationships.
>
> *Accept:* Ah, so... come to a realization of what reality *is* without judgment or resistance, and trust your ability to handle it.
>
> *Embrace:* Be grateful for lessons learned, character gained, and gifts brought to light.

AVOIDING THE FUTURE SNARE

We can go anywhere and do anything through the magical power of imagination. Imagination creates and, therefore, is a godlike quality. However, imagination also has a shadow side. It loves to whisk us into the future where it's easy to be ensnared by fear. While it's wise to allow what is, it's equally wise not to imagine what is *not*. Sure, it's fun to bask in uplifting scenarios and enjoy the anticipation of upcoming celebrations. But so often forays into the future are more foreboding than fun. During future-thought, we can easily get caught in what-ifs—*What if I fail? What if he leaves me?*—and wouldn't-it-be-awfuls—

Wouldn't it be awful if my kids turn out horribly? Wouldn't it be awful if I had to stay in this job forever?

Weakness and fear are by-products of scary future projections, whereas strength is more often than not alive and well in the present moment.

I resonate with the pithy statement, "Wherever you are, be there!" Right here, right now is the only home we have. At home in the empowered present is where we sincerely connect with our selves and our loved ones. My friend Kathy, who has been living with an unpredictable form of cancer for over a year, says she's a different person now. "I'm much more *here* than I used to be. I was always somewhere else... I could fake being present, but I didn't really see the people I was with. Really, they sort of annoyed me. Now, I truly see the person in front of me. I'm much more attentive, and each minute, each person, each animal... and me... we're all so precious now."

Kathy spent the first few weeks after her diagnosis trapped in a terrifying future, unable to do much but weep. With the help of a wise therapist, she decided to allow cancer, and all it entails, to be a reality, but to keep her thoughts and attention in the present moment as much as possible. She's gotten darned good at it, and I've never known her to be stronger. Or more loving or appreciative.

During your day…

- ✧ Use your magical imagination to delight in the moment.
- ✧ Notice when you have strayed into a future snare and gently return to the present. Anchor yourself there by carefully examining and appreciating an object close to you, even if it's a simple paperclip.
- ✧ Delete what-ifs and wouldn't-it-be-awfuls from your mind's hard drive.

The point of power is always in the present moment.
—LOUISE HAY

LOOSENING THE GRIP

Resistance is counterproductive, yet it's often our go-to reaction when something or someone crosses our path causing us to gasp and say versions of, "Can you *believe* that/it/her/him/them!?!" And, we're off, resisting mightily and usually righteously. Maybe we *are* right, but it doesn't matter. Right or wrong, resistance clamps its big fist around your lifeforce channels, cutting off joy, tolerance, understanding, peace of mind, and love, to name only a few things it blocks. If that isn't bad enough, resistance attracts to you exactly the kind of energy you are resisting. Imagine a popcorn kernel stuck in your throat. Until it's dislodged, your mind is thinking about it; your body is working to release it; and you're frustrated, uncomfortable, and maybe a little scared. On a mental and emotional level, resistance gets stuck in your craw, continually annoying you and grabbing your attention. Resistance is so grabby it can close down our hearts (metaphorically) and cloud our vision until we are neither clear-headed nor open-hearted.

While meditating this morning, I noticed myself fretting about a family situation, mildly resisting the pain it was causing my loved one—and me, to a lesser extent. All of a sudden, the word *ALLOW* appeared in my mind, flashing in technicolor on a movie marquee. I laughed and then literally felt my jaw unclench. Seconds later, I realized my entire body was relaxing with a soothing, sighing/sagging sensation. Ah… resistance melting in the spacious warmth of allowing.

Because this was not a large-scale or long-term resistance, acceptance followed quickly. Embracing is yet to come.

During your day, week, life...

- ✧ If journaling is helpful to you, jot down any resistance you may be holding. Muse on it. Sometimes simply becoming aware of resistance allows It to transform.
- ✧ If the feeling doesn't change, have a wise, compassionately nonattached subpersonality play the role of Observer. I often find it helpful to distance myself from the drama of resistance.

✧ Come up with your own creative ways to loosen the grip of resistance.

> *Your resistance is what slows down things*
> *for you. Allow instead of resisting.*
> —ROXANA JONES

BOWING TO IMPERMANENCE

I'm not a person who thinks change is fun and adventurous. I'm the gal who uses graph paper to figure out where furniture goes in a new house, places it where we like it, and leaves it there. This behavior sounds boring as I write it, but it feels sweet, secure, and homey to me. My favorite mug shows a cat sliding down a surface leaving claw marks above her. It says, "Everything I've ever let go of has claw marks all over it." Thankfully, with change as my life-long tutor, and aging as its accomplice, I have finally been able to forge a fairly comfortable alliance with change.

Because words are an avenue of understanding for me, being able to blend the inevitability of change with the Buddhist concept of impermanence is helping me along the road to embracing both.

I'm not there yet. My head accepts the fact of impermanence, but my heart chooses not to think about it often. My intellect knows everything is temporary and believes it to be an excellent choice of the Creator's. But, frankly, I still have a ways to go before the *truth* of impermanence saturates all the cells of my being. I have moments of saturated knowing, especially when basking in the disarming smile of a baby or admiring simple or intricate sandcastles knowing they will be gone after high tide. Although I'm still in the process of embracing impermanence, one day my heart will be able to bow completely to its actuality because I trust Buddhist teacher Thich Nhat Hanh's hypothesis: "Once we recognize that all things are impermanent, we have no problem enjoying them. In fact, real peace and joy are only possible when we see clearly into the nature of impermanence." I'd certainly enjoy increased peace and joy, wouldn't you?

Change and impermanence are the apex of what *is*. Are you able to embrace them both or, like me, are you still in the process of allowing, accepting, and assimilating their reality? I firmly believe when we can fully embrace change and impermanence, we will be stronger and wiser than we think possible.

During your day…

- ✧ Look at those you love with the eyes of impermanence. Does it change your perspective? Possibly make them more precious?
- ✧ Do the same with yourself.

- ✧ Go through pictures of yourself from babyhood to now. Ponder the impermanent *and* the eternal qualities of your selves.
- ✧ Cherish eternal, impermanent you.

> *Impermanence is a principle of harmony. When we don't*
> *struggle against it, we are in harmony with reality.*
>
> —Pema Chodron

ACCEPTING IS EMPOWERING

One of the reasons acceptance is empowering is that it alleviates irritation. The constant irritation of resisting what *is* can grind strength to oblivion and completely destroy balance and equilibrium, whereas acceptance grounds us in the reality of here and now, which is the only place we can find true happiness and healing. The acceptance I'm talking about is not giving up. Nor is it capitulation, submission, or defeat. Neither is it denial or acquiescence. The acceptance we're exploring is not wussy. On the contrary, it is wise and empowering.

When asked what made her such a strong woman, Elizabeth shared, "I'm a strong woman because, after much rage, resistance, and grief I've come to compassion and acceptance." Elizabeth shared a story she'd written with me. Bittersweetly entitled "Titan Descending," it sketched the decline of her intelligent, fun-loving, and thoughtful husband—a man who could "do anything" according to himself—into a man riddled with anxiety and drained of energy. "My rock became porous and vulnerable," Elizabeth confided. Both Elizabeth and her husband denied reality for many months, each blaming the other for changes both loathed. When denial eventually passed, resistance and grief were "making me a crazy, irritable bitch." This is when Elizabeth chose to come to therapy.

When you need to accept loss of any kind, grief is naturally present. Loss, whether of a dream, desire, or the death of a loved one, deserves to be mourned. Grieving allows you to honor and move *through* your sadness and eventually move *into* appreciation for what is. From that balanced place, you have the strength to make needed changes. As sadness, disappointment, and anger subside and acceptance comes to the fore, relief is palpable and gratitude is able to replace resistance.

A great bonus I've discovered about acceptance is that, when I accept a BIG disappointment or challenge, the small ones become less inflamed. I imagine that is Maya Angelou's idea "If you don't like something, change it. If you can't change it, change your attitude" playing out in real life.

During your day...

✦ Acceptance is a many layered, often difficult process. If you find yourself stuck, give yourself the gift of sharing your process with a wise, understanding friend, therapist, or group.

✧ Loss is inevitable. Allow yourself the healing power of grief.

✧ Please be gentle with yourself as you open your heart, mind, and soul to becoming skilled in the art of acceptance.

> *We cannot change anything until we accept it.*
> *Condemnation does not liberate, it oppresses.*
>
> —CARL JUNG

DOING IT YOUR WAY

The right way to do such and so is... You should do it this way... Anything worth doing is worth doing right.... I don't know about you, but I'm tired of being told there's a right way to do something. Who says? And, who cares, no matter *who* says?

For more decades than I choose to remember, my New Year's resolutions included "Meditate each day." Most years I managed to meditate in what I'd learned was the right way, for a few days, but it felt more obligatory than satisfying. A couple of years ago, I chucked ancient and modern wisdom on how to meditate correctly and began my own version. My morning time has many variations; among them are:

- ✧ **Medi-pray**: Pretty obvious what this version entails.
- ✧ **Medi-play**: Time to cavort with and be cared for by angels, guides, and helper Beings (whom I share about in chapter 12).
- ✧ **Medi-fray**: A place to fall apart and knit frayed ends together.
- ✧ **Medi-practice**: Using practices I'm learning during intuition training.
- ✧ **Medi-write**: Capturing ideas, insights, and haiku floating in the silence.
- ✧ **Snoozeitate**: Sweet dream snippets often accompany this favorite form.

When I was dutifully trying to meditate in the correct way, five minutes felt like an eternity. Doing it my way, an hour flies by. My medi-Sue's-way times are fun, calming, strengthening, inspiring, and sometimes powerful. I'm addicted and loving it!

Is there anything you want to try but aren't sure you can do it right? Painting? Music lessons? Have an honest, possibly life-changing conversation? Do something entrepreneurial? Meditate? Get a job? Quit a job? How about allowing yourself to do it *your* way!

Certainly, some things need to be done correctly—scuba diving, for example—but most endeavors have plenty of room for individuality, creativity, and innovation. If your way is authentic, comes from sincere desire, and does no harm, it is *your* right way. Allow yourself to go for it. Get inspired. Play....

During your day...

- ✧ If you are tired of or bored with something, ponder other ways of doing it.
- ✧ Imagine how you might blossom if you didn't let the *right* way get in *your* way.
- ✧ Love and support yourself no matter what you're doing, or not doing, no matter how you're doing, or not doing, it.

> *Promise me you'll always remember: You're braver than you believe, and stronger than you seem, and smarter than you think.*
>
> —CHRISTOPHER ROBIN TO WINNIE THE POOH
> (A. A. MILNE)

ALLOWING BYGONES TO BE GONE

A caveat: I know several wise women who dislike the expression "Let it go." My friend Sadie exclaims, "Go?! Go *where*?!" If you feel the same—which I sometimes do—please feel free to substitute "Allow" or "Let it be."

That said, letting go is one of the most loving gifts you can give yourself and others. Ironically, it's also one of the most difficult. Research shows that Mother Nature has wired our brains to register negative, fearful, and unpleasant experiences more deeply and vividly than it does positive, neutral, or pleasant ones. Being ultra-alert and holding negative experiences in the forefront of their minds helped ancient peoples survive, but doing so today actually dampens our ability to thrive. Not letting go is like watering the garden with your foot firmly planted on the hose.

NOT-SO-GOOD NEWS

- ✧ In the feast of life, the brain swallows negative experiences whole but only samples positive ones.
- ✧ Not letting go binds us to the original wound, regret, or circumstance.
- ✧ Holding on holds us hostage.

GOOD NEWS

- ✧ Realizing that letting go is hard *physiologically* as well as emotionally helps alleviate guilt. Being aware of the brain's tendency to heighten and hang on to the negative facilitates letting go of self-blame and/or shame.

- ✧ *Brains are retrainable.* Consciously *paying attention* to positive experiences helps your brain learn to register them more intensely. Noticing and absorbing positives alerts your brain to etch deeper pathways for them to travel. Creating new pathways takes time, but practice makes progress.
- ✧ Letting go *liberates us*, and others, from being stuck in the resin of past grievances, disappointments, and hurts.

While it may sound counterintuitive, letting go honors your experiences. In lieu of discounting feelings, I believe the very feminine practice of letting go and moving on acknowledges the strength, resilience, wisdom, and compassion gleaned from searing experiences. Very importantly, letting go allows you to return to the here and now where real life and connection reside. Letting go is freeing—energetically, emotionally, mentally, and physically.

During your day…

- ✧ Choose one fragment of stuck energy to let go of. Imagine how it will feel to be liberated from the hold this energy has on you.

✧ Be deeply aware of, and soak up, happiness, joy, and contentment to help your brain build superhighways for the Positive.

✧ Write a list entitled "I Am Free From" and jot down things to release.

Liberation is an act of love and a foundation for freedom.

AGING, A CUMULATIVE VENTURE

Refusing to accept the reality of aging can leach the strength right out of you. Resistance of any kind drains energy reserves, and resistance to aging is especially unproductive for a couple of obvious reasons. One, it's a fact. Two, very few of us are hoping to speed up the alternative. Since we've been aging from day one, we might as well embrace the reality, accumulate the wisdom, and have a rewarding time along the way.

At closer-to-eighty-than-I-ever-imagined-being, I feel younger than I did at thirty—not physically, of course, but definitely in outlook, attitude, and freedom of expression. I love thinking of myself, and my contemporaries, as chronologically gifted and fully agree with Madeleine L'Engle's belief that "The great thing about getting older is that you don't lose all the other ages you've been." How great is that? Just a thought away are all the yous that ever were. All your ages combine to create the accrued wisdom, compassion, and humor you've gathered along the way. Truly a treasure trove of growth and courage.

"Old" is definitely looking and acting younger and more vibrant than it used to, and psychological and spiritual awareness is playing a big role in our changing view of aging. Only recently has ancient esoteric spiritual wisdom and pioneering scientific research been available to the general population. As a result, we are much more aware of the body/mind connection, our inner selves, and the effect of attitude on everything. The cumulative information and understanding available in my generation alone are staggering.

Past self-fulfilling assumptions that aging meant decline and poor health are being revised and, as a result, vitality, contribution, and contentment are on the rise.

Let's join the trend and allow ourselves to concentrate on the treasures accumulated through the years rather than the losses and limitations natural and necessary to the process.

During your day...

⋄ Have fun and be a little sassy about aging. Looking at my body, which is melting southward daily, the word *SAG* came to mind. I decided to have it stand for something powerful: **s**agacious **a**nd **g**rateful is my acronym.

✧ Similar to writing in a gratitude journal, acknowledge a wisdom, insight, or gem you've gleaned today. Regular acknowledgment can become a personal treasure chest.

Aging is not lost youth but a new stage
of opportunity and strength.
—BETTY FRIEDAN

COMING OF AGE

Primal feelings are normal in relation to our children. Grown in the center of our selves or adopted from the yearnings of our hearts, children are the ultimate cocreation with Source. Motherhood catapults us into a maze of unknowns with every nerve, neurosis, and heartstring electrified on occasion. Our children are walking, back-talking embodiments of our energy. Naturally and necessarily, we get attached. And, before we know it, they leave. Also natural and necessary. A "Birth and Release" law of nature. Whether you are thrilled with the emptying nest or having a hard time adjusting, life is changing. Fresh facets of yourself are beckoning. Not only are the kids coming of age, so are you.

While the empty nest is a good example, coming of age certainly doesn't limit itself to mothers and has much more to do with circumstances than it does age. Each of us is given the opportunity to come of age many times during a lifetime. When life takes a turn, you move, a relationship ends, illness or injury interrupts plans, you enter a coming-of-*that*-age period. Because there are countless unknowns in any new phase, strength and courage are required, as are patience and compassion for yourself. During times of change—internal and external—we are called to redefine ourselves and invite previously unripe aspects of ourselves into the open. Change takes time. Allowing yourself time isn't easy but is necessary in order for transformation to unfold organically and rightfully. Just as it takes nine months for a baby to be ready for birth, internal rebirth also takes time. Frustratingly, there's no way to know the due date.

Also making it difficult to allow coming-of-*new*-age the time it needs is that often diametrically different feelings coexist—scared as hell riding tandem with excited and enlivened. Making it fun and creative helps pass the time. My latest coming-of-age chapter was embracing Cronedom. A fun part of my process was painting a self-portrait entitled "The Dowager Dragon." Being born in the year of the dragon, I like the symbology, and her cartoon quality and fiery expression that say "Just try it, buddy!" tickle me.

During your day…

✦ Remember coming-of-age times you've experienced. Congratulate yourself on the strength you had to redefine yourself.

- ✧ If you're in a time of change, mindfully be gentle, patient, and kind to yourself. If you do not need to change right now, please do the same.
- ✧ Have fun, get creative, and be amused and amazed by your many incarnations.

We are so many different people in one lifetime.
—DEBORAH LAWRENSON

ADAPTING TO THE INEVITABLE AND UNAVOIDABLE

Life is a continual spiral of transition and change. Control is illusion. Yes, we can control a few things for a little while. For instance, most of you can hold your breath for several seconds—or minutes if you're a free diver or yogini—but eventually you must breathe again. Outside circumstances, other people, and our own automatic brain reactions are not easily controlled no matter how determined we are or hard we try. Thankfully, with mindfulness and practice, we can find the strength to control many of our attitudes, thoughts, actions, responses, and choices. Many of these alterations come into play when adapting to something unwanted yet unavoidable.

Jewish poet Judah Halevi wrote "'Tis a fearful thing to love what death can touch," yet we courageous humans choose to love anyway.

I have a suspicion women feel free to choose love *and* loss because we intuitively know we are masterful adapters. Experience has shown us how well we can adjust to new conditions, including death. My son Mike asked, "Isn't adaptation actually a matter of survival?" Yes, he's right. In fact, *Survival of the most **adept at adapting*** is a complementary addition to the *survival of the fittest* adage.

The more adept at adapting we are, the happier, stronger, and more productive we can be.

My friend Kaida has chronic fatigue syndrome and hereditary spinal issues. A former firefighter now in her fifties, Kaida has had to make major adaptations in her lifestyle. As is true for many people with chronic conditions, for Kaida, adapting is a daily exercise in awareness and acceptance of what her body is capable of in the moment.

Adapting and grieving walk hand in hand. It is essential you allow yourself to grieve when adapting to loss and lifestyle changes. *A grief concealed is a grief congealed.* The intense energy of grief can heal only when allowed to flow, be released, and transform in its right time and way. Allowing and accepting grief help you uncover the best mode of expression for you. Because we are easily blindsided and isolated by grief, seeking support and guidance while experiencing it is a wise decision.

During your day...

✧ Give yourself credit for the myriad ways you have adapted in the past.

- ❖ Allow yourself to grieve loss and change. Express grief's energy in constructive and helpful ways—with trustworthy and compassionate people when helpful.
- ❖ Be kind and patient with yourself.

> *Time heals almost everything. Give time time.*
> —REGINA BRETT

HONORING WHERE YOU ARE

Even though this book is about strength, please understand that sometimes we simply cannot be, feel, or act strong. For the vast majority of us, those times are few and fleeting. If and when strength vanishes, the wisest and strongest thing you can do is honor where you are!

I am a strong ol' broad, as strong as my home state's Missouri mule. However, a few years ago a sequence of deep personal losses culminated with me spending the beautiful months of May and June deeply involved with my dear friend Jean's diagnosis and death. Jean was one of those rare individuals whom everyone liked. She was a model, mentor, friend, chosen big sister, confidant, and laughing buddy to me. Being with her from the first shocking view of her PET scan through the actual moment of death caused me to run the gamut of emotions. I vacillated between periods of open-heartedness so meaningful that I completely resonated with Walt Whitman's statement "I am larger, better than I thought; I did not know I held so much goodness" and times of soul-searing rage.

Already drained from the preceding string of losses, my physical, emotional, mental, and spiritual circuits blew. Any semblance of equilibrium evaporated, and I was left in the wreckage of my own well-being. Everything and everyone, even my little dog, Lily, grated on my nerves. It took every smidgen of energy I had to keep from acting as bitchy and irritable as I felt. Life was shrouded in a dank, gray mist, and my attitude could be summarized in three words: *I don't care.*

After recovering, I created an acronym—*HUG*—standing for what helped me come out of the emotional wasteland. This is practical stuff that works for intermittent, circumstance-driven, out-of-balance times. (Chronic depression and persistent feelings of "I don't care" are very different things. HUG may help but by no means cure them.)

H   Honor where you are.
    Honoring means acknowledging, allowing, and
    accepting the reality and, very possibly, the underlying
    wisdom of what you are experiencing right now.
    Honoring does *not* include slathering yourself with
    guilt or shame, denying how you feel, or acting out in
    unloving ways to yourself or others.

U Utilize support that helps.

Sharing honestly with a few trusted friends helped me tremendously.

Utilizing excessive booze, food, or excessive *anything* doesn't work.

Overutilizing any one avenue of support until they burn out doesn't work.

G Gently, Gently, Gently.

I know I beat the "gentle drum" incessantly, but being gentle with yourself works; beating yourself up does not.

During your day...

❖ *HUG* yourself consistently and compassionately.

> *May you love yourself gently and well no matter where you are or what you are feeling.*

10

CHOOSING WISELY

Today I am choosing to love myself because
I want to love others more purely.

—Colleen George

Choice is perhaps our most vital freedom. We sometimes start sentences with "Given a choice…" In reality, almost every waking moment offers myriad choices. Many are small and inconsequential, whereas others are life changing. Together, all choices create the pattern of your life, revealing how your life is trending.

Choice is a blessing. Do your choices trend toward being blessings by enhancing strength, increasing wisdom, regaining balance, developing empowerment, spreading kindness, and promoting self-love and love of others? If so, I am encouraged and feel hope for Mother Earth and her children everywhere. If your choices have not been gentle and self-loving, they can begin to be from this moment on. It is up to you.

As you are well aware by now, I have a couple of favorite soapboxes from which I write and, increasingly, live. One is the yearning for feminine and masculine qualities and power to come into balance and harmony within all people and the world. The other is the belief that loving ourselves into wholeness and closer to holiness is our souls' task. Doing so allows us to be open-hearted and able to share our innate wisdom and kindness with others and the world.

Choice is your power point. You can choose to embrace and act from your intrinsic feminine qualities. Very importantly, choose to love yourself. Self-loving people express and elevate heart energy, create balance, and abet healing. As the Buddha said, "If you truly loved yourself, you could never hurt another."

LEANING TOWARD THE LIGHT

As mentioned earlier, everything we do, think, and feel is on a continuum from fear to love or, for the sake of this meditation, from dark to light.

Fear _____ Love

Dark _____ Light

Heavy _____ Buoyant

Obscure _____ Transparent

With its emphasis on connection, forgiveness, and inclusion, feminine energy leans toward the light while also being able to courageously be present when experiencing darkness herself or compassionately caring for others who are wrestling with darkness. Whether in miniscule or mighty amounts, each choice we make either adds light or increases darkness.

By her own admission, Melanie, our sassy dog groomer—who traded a responsible corporate position for a four-footed clientele to "save her sanity"—has a quick Irish temper, especially while driving. After a couple of scary incidents with other drivers, Melanie decided to stop letting her temper put her and other drivers in danger. She set an intention not to act on her temper and put a reminder on her dashboard that says, "DO NOT ENGAGE!" Who knows? Melanie's reminder may be a lifesaver. It's certainly made driving more peaceful, she says.

Intention is our ally. It actually helps us build inner strength by creating a plan and a focal point for change. For instance, if you set the intention to speak more kindly to yourself, your brain is likely to give you a little ping. Hopefully, *before* you badmouth yourself, but definitely after. Intention is a reminder in your brain — similar to your phone—to help you lean toward the light. And talking to yourself in the way you talk to a friend is a huge move toward the light of love.

One great way to lean toward the light is simply to smile. As my son Brett says, "At the intersection of every path you cross, plant smiles." Smiles are heart-lifters and excellent energy-uppers.

During your day...

✦ In what ways would you like to lean toward the light?
  Jot them down. If you feel strongly enough about
  leaning in a certain way, set a gentle intention to do so.

✦ What kindness can you begin giving yourself? As if you
  were your own BFF, provide it.

✦ Give yourself credit for at least one way you already
  lean toward the light and spread love.

If you want to do something for world peace, cultivate kindness,
stop hating, and have hope for all individuals including yourself.
—PATRICIA SUN

LETTING GO OF EFFORTING

Tomorrow is my birthday. I *love* birthdays. This year, I will have
lived five years longer than my mother did, and that alone brings up a
multitude of feelings. Paramount among them is gratitude for countless
blessings and for friends and family whom I can count on. Along with
intense thankfulness comes a little musing about what might have been
and what is. One of the thoughts that bubbled up was how much of
my earlier life was spent *efforting*. Trying too hard to be perfect, to be
liked, to please others, to live up to unrealistic expectations, to be an

always-available friend, a sexy/fun wife, a compassionate and insightful therapist. I'm sure you can add a list of your own areas of efforting to the list.

The kind of efforting I'm talking about is different from the desire to do your best or give something your all. When doing comes from love, enthusiasm, and desire, it is fulfilling and soul-feeding. The *efforting* I'm referring to is rooted in fear, steeped in anxiety, and reeking of expectation. This type of guilt-ridden effort is driven by neediness and sabotages your strength and dampens your spirit.

For example, I tried so hard to be a good... who am I kidding? I thought I should be a *perfect* mother and stepmother. Looking back, I realize not trusting myself or my parenting abilities caused me to fall into the effort abyss. Trying too hard often got in the way of really enjoying my kids as much as I would have if I'd been more relaxed and less worried. I'm not beating myself up now, just musing. Hindsight has given me perspective, and I truly believe I did the best I could. Thankfully, I'm making progress in letting go of efforting, and as a result, the kids and I have an easy relationship. Plus, I just plain enjoy life more.

Musing about past lack of trust reminds me to upgrade today's trust in myself to the same level I have for "my birthday" daffodils. I know they will bloom anew each season, even if there is snow. I had my first glimpse of spring daffodils today, and seeing them lifted my heart. When we give ourselves the love and trust we deserve, we also bloom anew and lift hearts in the process.

During your day…

- ✧ If you notice yourself efforting in an uncomfortable way, mindfully stop and ask yourself why. Is your reason rooted in love or based in fear, guilt, or need?
- ✧ Consciously relax and allow blooming to take place naturally.

Anything done with, and from, love is usually good enough.

ACCEPTING THE PARADOX OF PERFECTION

I believe we *are* perfect. All of us, you and me, and everyone else. Spiritually, as a soul. A definition of perfection I resonate with is "free from any flaw or defect in condition or quality; faultless." Although I don't see the Sue writing this meditation in that list, I *do* believe with all my heart that the definition does pertain to the soul animating my human self. As it does yours.

If human perfection is an unreachable star, why do we bludgeon ourselves with the impossible dream of achieving it? For me, as a kid, I got the idea that being perfect was expected of me. I believed the payoff for perfection would be warm fuzzies such as love, acceptance, and parental pride as well as protection from rejection, anger, and criticism.

Perfection meant I'd never be a disappointment to myself or those I cared about and counted on. This, of course, left me pretty darned disappointed much of my life.

Over the years, I've come to believe one of the reasons my soul chose to come here is to experience imperfection and learn to feel love and compassion for myself and others, as imperfect as we are. Although I don't have empirical evidence to back up my theory, I do have an ever-increasing sense of *knowingness* about it, and that's good enough for me.

Choosing to be at peace with imperfection didn't come easily or early. Until the last few years, I think I clung to the illusion of human perfection because I was afraid letting it go could lead to giving myself a free pass, a Get Out of Jail Free card. Without such a lofty goal, would I lazily stop growing, learning, and evolving? Exactly the opposite is happening. Freed from the tyranny of perfection and the shame of failure, I'm more loving toward myself and others and much more eager to learn from the experiences at hand.

To me, the paradox of perfection is that we're never going to get there, although we already are. Because you (and all of us) carry a spark of the Divine Beloved within your core, perfection is your Essence.

During your day…

❖ Cherish the divine spark within.

❖ Love yourself as you are.

❖ Be amused by your imperfections; most are endearing.

The spark divine dwells in thee: let it grow.
—ELLA WHEELER WILCOX

CARING OR OVER-CARING?

A caveat: I know chronic caretaking issues are extremely complex and put some of you in untenable situations. I've been there and, as a result, understand that *killing the caretaker* is not a wise choice. If this is happening to you, please find allies and other solutions as quickly as possible. Advocating for yourself when you and others expect you to do more than is healthy for you takes an incredible amount of inner strength and resolve. Setting limits and boundaries can be very, very challenging. Nonetheless, self-care is a *must*.

To be clear, I'm not addressing crisis caretaking here. For instance, the teenage son of friends suffered heart failure three weeks ago. His mom didn't leave the hospital for two weeks, which was understandable and exactly what she needed to do to care for herself. I am addressing a chronic tendency to over-care and be obsessively concerned about some people and situations.

Caring for others and being cared for yourself are essential to your sense of well-being and feelings of connectedness. Knowing if your caring is realistic and balanced lies in how you feel. Balanced caring provides a sense of purpose, stimulates heart energy, and contributes to good health. It can be energizing even when you are physically worn out.

On the other hand, if caring leaves you feeling burdened and exhausted or closed-hearted and taken advantage of, chances are you have fallen into over-caring.

Kindly and respectfully, ask yourself the following questions:

- Do I carry all the responsibility for caring for (*person or situation*)?
- Do I feel blame, guilt, or responsibility for another's decisions, life, or hardships?
- Do think I know what they/it *should* do or be?
- Do I lose sleep worrying about this person or situation?
- Am I exhausted, anxious, angry, and irritable?

"Yes" answers indicate changes are needed. The tendency to over-care suggests harsh and unrealistic expectations about what you *should* do, be, and feel in order to be a loving woman.

During your day...

- Tuck your tendency to over-care into your heart. Gently breathe into your heart. As you inhale, affirm, "I love myself." While exhaling, say, "Just as I am."
- Tuck a person or situation you tend to over-care into your heart. Breathe into your heart and imagine each breath surrounding them/it with love. Inhaling,

say, "I love you." Exhaling, affirm, "I trust you and your wisdom."

✧ Allow the rhythm of your breath to soothe and relax your heart.

A measure of balance is wise… as we seek to comfort another, promote our causes, or advance in our relationships.
—HEARTMATH INSTITUTE

LIVING AT YOUR OWN PACE

Giving yourself permission to live at your own pace is one of the wisest choices you can make. Some of us are naturally Energizer Bunnies while others are lava flows. Some are convection ovens and others slow cookers. Until a few years ago, I was an Energizer Bunny—so much so that my ill mother once exclaimed, in a semi-irritated tone, "Sue, you have more energy than anyone I know." I'm an Aries, born in the year of the dragon, was a single mom of two kids, and then a mom/stepmom of four with an energetic husband, a career, four dogs, and a cat. Darn good thing I was energetic. Now, I'm a moderately energetic little ol' lady in tennis shoes who loves solitude and quiet pursuits like art, writing, and SoulCollage. Although I still have spurts of high energy, I've changed.

At any given stage of your life, you have a pace and capacity for stimuli that works optimally for you. Pace and stimuli tolerance can vary according to circumstances, stress, and health. If you are an introverted HSP—highly sensitive person—you may be able to hike endlessly but need to take concerts or big gatherings in small doses. The trick to pacing yourself is being mindful of who you authentically are, and how fast and furiously you are comfortable living, *right now*. And then allow and accept your reality and give yourself permission to act accordingly.

Even if your lifestyle requires more energy and a faster pace than you are comfortable with, it's vital you honor the toll it takes on your well-being and find pockets of time to live at your personal pace. Take care of yourself by carving out spaces of underwhelm, simplicity, and adequate sleep. Find times in which to gather strength, recuperate, and replenish reservoirs. Or, if you are an Energizer Bunny in the midst of a family of tortoises, regularly pick up your personal pace in ways that match your energy level.

For many of us, rushing is wearing, whereas simplicity invites serenity, but we still live a life of way-too-much and way-too-fast. To help restore equilibrium, explore extricating yourself from overload in order to create a more balanced, you-friendly existence.

During your day…

- ❖ Become aware of whether or not you are living at your preferred, or needed, pace. Gently act on your awareness.
- ❖ If energy outgo exceeds energy inflow, how might you restore balance?
- ❖ Sleep is the best physician and a great shrink. Prioritize getting enough every opportunity you have.

> *There's a difference between challenging yourself and overwhelming yourself. It's okay to go at your own pace.*
> —THE GOOD QUOTE

SUBSTITUTING CURIOSITY

The Persian poet Rumi invites us to a higher playing field when he says, "In this earth, in this soil, in this pure fertile field, let us not plant any seeds other than the seeds of compassion and love." It's easy to know what seeds of compassion and love are, and I bet you plant those multiple times daily. A compliment, eye contact, interested listening, and your willingness to stand up for someone are examples of love and compassion seeds. Centered in heart energy, the Divine Feminine in you generously sows these seeds regularly and almost automatically. But it's also really tempting to spread weed seeds.

On our way to the higher playing field, what if we chose *not* to plant weed seeds like judgment, shame, and blame, for instance, and substituted curiosity instead? Today in church, two women were talking relatively loudly while the visiting minister was speaking. My first thoughts were judgmental with a side of irritation. For some reason—maybe because it was church?—my thoughts converted to curiosity. *Hmmm, I wonder if they are deaf?* That simple switch from judgment to curiosity short-circuited the irritation, and I felt neutral. Truthfully, I was surprised how quickly and completely judgment and irritation dissipated.

The definition of curiosity is "a strong desire to know or learn something," which is a great attribute to cultivate. When tempted to join the barrage of negativity existing today, what if you substituted curiosity for righteousness, fear, or disgust? What if you simply refused to participate in sowing any seeds other than curiosity, compassion, or love? Personally, I would have the hardest time substituting curiosity when feeling criticized, misunderstood, or blamed. But what a relief it would be if I could become curious rather than wounded, fearful, or defensive. It'll be a stretch, but I'm going to go for it....

Who knows? Maybe curiosity can become an antidote for emotional inflammation of all kinds. Wouldn't it be rewarding if substituting curiosity for fear, in all its iterations, elicited clearer insights and generated deeper connections with others? Today's tiny experience showed me curiosity is conducive to acceptance and leads me to believe that, if used regularly, it can also create new feel-good synapses in our brains.

During your day…

- ✧ Deliberately choose to substitute curiosity at least once.
- ✧ Consciously, with gentle attention, plant a seed or two of compassion and love.

> *As I get older, the more I stay focused on the acceptance of myself and others, and choose compassion over judgment and curiosity over fear.*
>
> —TRACEE ELLIS ROSS

ADOPTING COMPASSIONATE NONATTACHMENT

> *He who binds to himself a joy*
>
> *Does the winged life destroy;*
>
> *But he who kisses the joy as it flies*
>
> *Lives in eternity's sunrise.*
>
> —WILLIAM BLAKE

In 1972, this Blake poem inspired me to begin my quest for joy and compassionate nonattachment although I was decades away from labeling or succeeding at either.

For most of my life, attachment was my middle name. I was attached to people, outcomes, self-image, and what others thought of me. I clung to plans, promises, expectations, the way things should and shouldn't be, and the way *I* should and shouldn't be. Then life turned upside down, and all my plans and future projections blew up in a volcano of hurt, rage, and desperation. It was truly one of the best things that ever happened to me because it broke my strangle-hold on, well, almost everything. It also taught me I could survive when life failed to match my hopes and expectations.

The shake-up of my life felt like being submerged in a sea of impermanence. I eventually bobbed to the surface and am continually learning to go with the natural flow of all things and respect the impermanence of all life. Now, thankfully, I can often look at disappointments and crises as chances to practice nonattachment and enjoy the peace of mind and sense of freedom it offers. A neutral "Ah, so"… has become a helpful response when faced with the desire to attach and control and manage and advise and… and… and.

For me, compassionate nonattachment is a state of mind inviting me to trust. In fact, in my journey, the main lesson in nonattachment is *trust.* By no longer clinging to my ideas of what *should* be, I'm learning to trust myself and what *is.* Trust has led me to the conviction that people I love, especially my hubby and kids, are completely capable of taking care of their own lives and things will work out. Nonattachment doesn't mean I don't care or am not available if someone needs me. It means I've stopped thinking I need to fix everyone and everything. It means I accept the fact I don't know what's best for others, am not responsible for their lives, and can enjoy and love myself, and them, as is.

During your day...

- ✧ Kiss the joy as it flies.
- ✧ Trust....

> *You are a child of the universe,*
> *No less than the trees and the stars;*
> *You have a right to be here.*
> *And whether or not it is clear to you,*
> *No doubt the universe is unfolding as it should.*
> —MAX EHRMANN, "DESIDERATA"

KICKING BUTT CONSTRUCTIVELY

Too often, we let people walk all over us. While discussing that reality, my friend Jane jokingly said, "I have footprints all over my face." We laughed, but it's not really funny or healthy. To come into full strength and power, we need to learn to kick butt compassionately and constructively.

While feminine energy is heartfelt and compassionate, it is also empowered and persistent. Feminine energy fights for what is best for everyone; therefore, it's necessary for her—and us—to kick butt sometimes. To reap the highest rewards and feel good about ourselves, we need to stay true to our values by kicking butt *constructively*.

I find the following steps helpful when the need arises:

- ✧ **Recognize**: Intense emotion such as hurt, anger, or disappointment often precedes the need to boot buns. Since it is rarely wise to act when feelings are inflamed, recognize the emotion. Acknowledge your feelings and accept their validity. Tell the kickee you need to step back and cool off.

- ✧ **Release**: In ways that resonate with you, soothe and work through feelings. Different approaches work for different emotions. Anger often needs to be expressed. Exercising, crying, screaming, and beating a bed with a tennis racket are ways to express. Hurt may need the comfort and company of friends. After feelings have calmed, imagine your grounding cord extending from the base of your spine into the center of Mother Earth. Send any emotional residue down the cord to be transformed and transmuted by the Mother.

✦ **Replace**: Replace released emotions with strength, resolve, courage, conviction, and a tangible plan about what needs to change and shift.

Kicking butt constructively includes:

✦ No *Blame* but necessary *Boundaries*
✦ No *Victimhood* but lots of *Courage, Resolve,* and *Self-responsibility*
✦ No *Threats* but clear *Consequences*

As an example, Patty's husband and dog-walker, George, had promised to keep their little dog away from a neighbor's dog who had attacked it three times. One day, by accident, Patty saw George and the two dogs together. She was furious, terrified for her dog's safety, and hurt by the blatant betrayal of a promise. Patty told George what she'd seen and that she needed time to calm down. It took a day before Patty felt like talking. At a time George and Patty agreed to, she shared her feelings and offered to take over dog-walking duty. She let him know it would take awhile before she could trust him again, and she might not be able to forgive him if he allowed their dog to be hurt.

During your day…

✧ If people try to leave footprints on your face, constructively kick their butts.

> *You get in life what you have the courage to ask for.*
> —OPRAH WINFREY

NOTICING MIRACLES

Whether we notice or not, miracles abound. Well, really, *if* we notice, miracles abound. Miracles can be tiny to humongous. Being aware of them buoys our spirits and fills our emotional reservoirs. The other day, my small miracle was noticing the little halo of cottonwood fluff on the head of a large robin as we made eye contact. Seeing him with his puffy adornment was uplifting in a couple of ways. It amused me and also helped me feel a tiny bit less annoyed with the ubiquitous, gunk-spreading cottonwoods behind our house.

A different miracle was huge for me. For a while I've known a neighbor was bad-mouthing me, and one woman, especially, seemed to have soured toward me as a result. Because it's terribly difficult for me if people see me in ways I know I'm not, I've been distraught by the situation. Very consciously I've made wise choices throughout this whole ordeal, but nothing I've done, or not done, has helped.

Therefore, acceptance has been my only option. And I have. But it still hurts. Driving into the neighborhood recently, I was feeling upset and thinking about Wayne Dyer's adage "What other people think about me is none of my business" when there she was, the soured woman. I waved and she smiled… for the first time in months. I've seen her one time since, and she smiled again. I don't need to understand what's changed; I only feel a deep gratitude for the healing I'm experiencing and for the miraculous timing of that first smile.

Life can be abrasive. Making the wise choice to notice daily miracles is balm to the raw places in our hearts and souls. Little miracles can be a dollop of grace amid harsh reality. Minute miracles lift our hearts and lighten our attitude. A miracle a day helps keep the doldrums at bay.

During your day…

✧ Be on the lookout for miniscule miracles—a heart-shaped prickly pear pad or synchronicities of any kind.

✧ Create a little miracle of your own. Tell others how much they have impacted your life, send an anonymous gift, compliment a stranger, write a haiku, make amends.

✧ Have fun inviting miracles to multiply by noticing them.

> *Today, look for a small sign, a small miracle, a*
> *small thing of beauty that will connect you to*
> *the SOURCE of all beauty and miracles.*

> —ANNIE KAGAN

INVITING JOY

Recently, riding on a motorcycle with my son on the Pacific Coast Highway, I was filled with the quiet joy of being exactly where I wanted to be at the time. Being at the births of my grandsons swelled my heart with joy. Feeling the presence of angels and guides in quiet moments causes joy to ooze warmly through my being. Writing a great sentence or a meaningful haiku also brings me joy. When the kids were living at home, seeing them loving and helping each other gave me joy. Watching them be uniquely themselves elicited joy, and still does.

Joy is a state of open-hearted well-being, gratitude, and happiness. Joy can be quiet and calm or rowdy and energized. It has a childlike quality and is equally wondrous when shared with others or savored in solitude. Joy is the song of our souls.

In my experience, joy has three fundamental forms:

- ✧ **Momentary**: Fleeting moments of beauty and grace that pass unnoticed unless we are present in the moment and able to pay attention
- ✧ **Enduring**: An attitude of gratitude for specific and universal blessings and beauty
- ✧ **Unexplainable**: Spiritual and mystical knowingness not linked to circumstances

Even though countless joys are longing to bless you each day, they can be obscured by veils of fear, judgment, and self-criticism. Joy and judgment cannot coexist. In fact, negative attitudes and beliefs of any kind often keep us from noticing and experiencing joy. Not because it isn't there, but because the cattle-prod-energy of the negative lures our attention away from joy. Therefore, as random as it may sound, I believe self-love and acceptance are the main invitations we can issue to joy. Once we can genuinely say, "Joy, come and bless me; I'm worthy of receiving you!" it will oblige. When...

When, what? When we are present in the here and now, when we pay attention, and when we *notice*. Joy doesn't wave a red flag to get your attention; she gently enters your sphere and invites you to melt into the bliss she is offering.

During your day...

- ❖ Court joy by gracing the present moment with your presence.
- ❖ Embrace and *know* you are worthy of joy and all the gifts she offers.
- ❖ Invite joy by loving and accepting your uniquely wonderful selves.
- ❖ Make a little sign: "Joy: Must be present to experience."

Joy is your origin and destination.
Joy is the outbreath of your soul.

11

EMBODYING STRENGTH

I would like to be known as an intelligent woman, a courageous
woman, a loving woman, a woman who teaches by being.
—MAYA ANGELOU

Women are strong, always have been, and always will be. Due to
eons of brainwashing exemplified by Virginia Woolf's description
"Women have served all these centuries as looking glasses possessing
the magic and delicious power of reflecting the figure of man at twice
its natural size," our main difficulty is accepting our amazing and
myriad strengths. In fact, many of us are prone to reflect the figures
of ourselves at about half their natural size. Thankfully, girls and
women are now being encouraged to know and show their strength,
but in the recesses of our psyches, the idea that we are to *support*
power rather than *be* empowered still persists.

For our own good and the benefit of our families, our culture, and
the world, you and I are called to embody the strength we naturally
possess, love ourselves to wholeness, and use all our innumerable
gifts unreservedly.

WELCOMING THE VIRGIN

The original definition of *virgin* was "a woman sufficient unto herself." The word itself comes from a Latin root meaning "strength, force, and skill" and was eventually appropriated as *virile* to apply to men.

In my work, I've been privileged to witness many women reclaim and act from their original virgin dynamism. For years, I led grief support groups. Within a safe circle of similarly grieving individuals, widows usually discovered a vast well of inner strength and resilience. Many were surprised at how resilient, creative, and accomplished they became when the need arose. Thankfully, we don't have to kill off husbands or partners in order to tap into our self-sufficiency. We can do so at any age, as a result of any circumstance, or simply because the time is right.

My first book was entitled *The Courage to Be Yourself,* and I wrote it because it was hard for me to be myself when it displeased others. Since the expectation to be whomever someone *else* wanted you to be was tattooed on the inside of my generation's soul, writing about being myself didn't magically make it happen. However, as I've ripened on the vine, I have also welcomed my inner virgin home. Happily, I didn't have to jettison the man in my life to regain her. Although, there were times…

My favorite reclaimed virgin is my ninety-one-year-old sister-in-law, Jo. She was raised in the Midwest, married young, and followed the blueprint of wife, mother, church lady, and all-round-wonderful-person she was expected to be. And did so happily. When her husband began a slow decent into diabetes and dementia, Jo started taking over all "manly" responsibilities. Among other things, Jo became financially capable, a whiz at making decisions, a fierce caregiver, and a persistent medical advocate.

When I asked Jo's permission to share her story, she said, "I think you're giving me too much credit. I just did what had to be done." That is *exactly* a woman's strength. We are exquisitely capable of doing what needs to be done.

During your day…

- ❖ If you automatically ask for help with things that are challenging for you, choose to try to do it yourself first.
- ❖ Muse about ways you'd like to be stronger, more gently forceful, and skilled. Try one or two.

There is nothing stronger than a woman in full power.

FINDING YOUR VOICE

The playground of life is littered with bullies of all kinds, and women are increasingly gathering together, growing up, and saying, "No Way!" The popular saying "Nevertheless, she persisted" prompted my friend Mary to comment, "Most of us are bona fide members of the Persisterhood." Very clever and so true. Together we are mighty. Individually we're not chopped liver either, but together we are unstoppable. As Isabel Allende declares, "I can promise you that women working together— linked, informed, and educated—can bring peace and prosperity to this forsaken planet." Yes, we can. And we need to.

It's so wonderful when women can stake claim to their voices in a humorous yet effective way. Madison, who works in a corporate setting, showed me a cartoon featuring five men and one woman sitting around a conference table. The man at the head of the table is saying, "That's an excellent suggestion, Miss Tiggs. Perhaps one of the men here would like to make it." Because similar dismissive experiences had happened to all the women in her department, Madison and her coworkers made copies of the cartoon and displayed it prominently at each of their cubicles. All the women agreed to silently point to the cartoon when experiencing unacceptable behavior from colleagues. Fortunately, their department manager—a woman—was all for the women's reminder. To everyone's credit, things improved.

Where do you feel you are currently trying to find your voice? At home? Work? In medical situations? Preschool? If you find it difficult to state your concerns, ask for what you want and need, or speak up in the face of mistreatment of yourself or others, you're not alone. Talking to friends, finding a support group, and going to therapy are often helpful avenues for discovering why you find speaking up challenging or, in some cases, terrifying. Comparing notes with other women can also be a rich source of how-tos for constructive communication. Working together, we can help each other find our voices.

During your day...

✧ Know that sharing your unique voice is an invaluable asset for your personal growth and the well-being of our beautiful planet.

✧ Give yourself permission to find your voice and use it compassionately, passionately, and constructively.

✧ You have a right to be heard and taken seriously. Persist!

> *A woman with a voice is by definition*
> *a strong woman. But the search to find*
> *that voice can be remarkably difficult.*
>
> —Melinda Gates

THRIVING

Musing about surviving versus thriving, I came up with a simple formula that, more often than not, helps me thrive. While similar to TLC, my acronym is *PLC*, which stands for "**p**urpose, **l**ove, and **c**reativity." In my experience, a combination of these three nouns can provide a pathway to thriving. Of course, you will have pathways that resonate with your soul, but just for fun, let's look at this one.

- ⬦ **Purpose**: You may have an overarching life's purpose. For years I thought mine was to love and serve. But something was not quite right. The idea was too grandiose, and I rarely felt I measured up. So, I decided to adopt bite-sized daily purposes such as being patient with a particular person, situation, or condition. You may choose being happy and spreading happiness as your life purpose. Anything is okay as long as it feels authentic and doable.
- ⬦ **Love**: Self-love is the seed from which all other love blooms. In light of that, discovering the best way to love yourself *in the current moment* is the heart of thriving.
- ⬦ **Creativity**: Creativity comes in every guise imaginable. Art, cooking, music, mothering, and theater are obvious avenues, but the scope of creativity is endless. When you lose track of time, you're being

creative. When someone says you've helped them,
creativity has had a voice. Anything that excites
or enlivens you is creativity singing and playing.
Whatever sparks enthusiasm, warms your heart, makes
you proud, pushes your laughter buttons, or brings you
alive has an element of creative expression.

The more you thrive and the higher your soul is invited to soar,
the stronger you will be.

During your day…

⬧ Without rush or worry, explore purpose. Do you
resonate with the idea of a life purpose, or are you
more of a daily purpose person? It's also okay to pass
on the idea of purpose, if that feels right.
✧ Spread seeds of love, first in your own heart's garden.
✧ What ember of creativity is longing for a little fanning in
order to warm your heart and make life juicier?

> *When we fulfill our function, which is to truly love ourselves*
> *and share love with others, then true happiness sets in.*
> —GABRIELLE BERNSTEIN

GIVING WITHOUT EXPECTATIONS

Have you ever made a kind gesture or given a gift and received no acknowledgment? I know it doesn't feel great, but what if we made a commitment to ourselves to give with no expectation of response, appreciation, or gold stars? How does that embody strength, you might be asking. To me, needing a response shows me whatever was given wasn't really a gift, but more of a barter—as in "I'll give you this and, in return, you owe me a positive response." Because I have a history of looking outside myself for validation and proof of my worthiness, I'm making a concerted effort to validate and love myself so completely that I don't *need* thanks and appreciation in order to believe in my own worthiness. I'm not there yet, but as I make headway in the ability to give without expectations—or even secret desires—of response, I feel immeasurably stronger. Plus my heart opens more fully, and I feel an inner joy in simply giving with no strings attached.

Since love is the only energy that brings lasting change, our sacred challenge is to love ourselves so well that outside validation, while nice and appreciated, is no longer *needed* to feel whole and happy and strong and useful. What if we could love ourselves deeply enough to heal the fears we carry within? I absolutely believe it's possible, as love is the true antithesis of fear. The more we love and value ourselves and our unique contributions, the less fear restricts our lives. The less fear we have, the closer we can come to unconditional loving. What a wonderful gift with which to bless ourselves and our beleaguered world.

During your day…

- ❖ Pay attention to all the little ways in which you make a difference in other people's lives. Shower yourself with credit and validation and, as far as possible, expect nothing from others in return.
- ❖ On the other hand, generously give others appreciation and gratitude when appropriate.
- ❖ Very consciously, open your heart to yourself several times a day. That may include acknowledging yourself for being courageous or comforting yourself when sad. You are the most important object of your love and support.
- ❖ Knowing that everything flows more freely from a deep well of self-love and acceptance, give both to yourself abundantly. And let it overflow onto others.

With great love and affection, consistently
fill your own cup to overflowing.

BREATHING GRATITUDE

Gratitude is a life-changing choice. Gratitude can lift your heart and sweeten even the saddest night. Gratitude is an elixir of light, able to lighten your attitude and plant seeds of hope in your soul. Gratitude is a decision that benefits your health, happiness, and relationships. Gratitude is as natural as breathing, but unlike breathing, gratitude does require a modicum of mindfulness and commitment.

A few years ago, Claudia and her sisters began a gratitude experiment. They jotted down a few things they were grateful for and emailed the list to each other at the end of the day. For Claudia, the gratitude practice is life changing, and it is creating an ever-deepening bond between the three sisters. Intrigue over some of the things listed elicits more phone calls between the sisters than ever before.

We control where our minds roam. Whether yours lives in the neighborhood of worry, fear, or judgment or inhabits the uplifting and hopeful realm of gratitude is up to you. If embracing gratitude is difficult for you, please be gentle and patient with yourself during the process. Old habits take awhile to dissipate, and new ones take time to become rooted in consciousness.

Practice makes progress. To inhabit the state of gratitude, notice small blessings and remember to feel thankful for them. Choosing gratitude as an overriding quality in your life allows you to recognize, even in the midst of calamity, that there is usually something to be thankful for in the moment. Breath, for instance.

Having an attitude of gratitude does for the spirit what pumping iron and exercise do for the body. It builds strength and stimulates a sense of well-being.

During your day…

- ✧ Set a reminder—in your mind or on your phone—for a few times a day. When it chimes, become aware of your breath. With each inhale and exhale cycle, visualize someone for whom you are grateful. Allow appreciation for them to warm your heart.
- ✧ Do the same exercise for some *thing* you are grateful for.
- ✧ Be grateful for at least one thing about yourself, or your Self, each day.

> *Not for everything that's been given to you can you really be grateful. So the key when people ask, can you be grateful for everything? No, not for everything, but in every moment.*
> —BROTHER DAVID STEINDL-RAST

BEING A SELF-HEALER

Early Hawaiians, and many other Polynesian cultures, practiced Ho'oponopono to bring families and communities into balance, harmony, and health. Hawaiian dictionaries define Ho'oponopono as (1) "to put to rights" and (2) "mental cleansing; family conferences in which relationships were set right through prayer, discussion, confession, repentance, mutual restitution, and forgiveness." The original fourteen-step practice was used by Dr. Ihaleakala Hew Len, Hawaiian therapist, to heal an entire ward of criminally insane patients without ever counseling them. Over the course of three years, Dr. Hew Len studied patients' charts, honored their connectedness with him and all beings and circumstances, and then healed himself. Because healing needs originate in our subconscious minds, and all minds are connected, Dr. Hew Len believes the patients healed because he healed his mind and heart. This sheds an interesting light on Gandhi's teaching "Be the change you wish to see in the world," doesn't it?

Personally, I have experienced amazing results using a simplified variation Dr. Hew Len created more recently. His Ho'oponopono practice is a four-step method of Repentance, Forgiveness, Gratitude, and Love based on the concept of oneness and the interconnectedness of everyone and everything. The four central prayer/mantras are

- ✧ *I'm sorry.*
- ✧ *Please forgive me.*
- ✧ *Thank you.*
- ✧ *I love you.*

The following meditative practice is best used within the quiet of your own heart and mind and not as a face-to-face way of making amends. The key to the Ho'oponopono practice is *Presence*. The healing power lies in being emotionally, mentally, and spiritually present while repeating the prayers. The order of the phrases is not important; whatever resonates with your heart is okay. Say them over and over. Mean it. Feel it.

During your day...

- ✧ **Step 1**: "I'm sorry." (Repentance)
  Although you are encouraged to say the mantra when you don't consciously understand a feeling of discomfort or dis-ease, I often find it helpful to have a who, what, where, and when to focus on. For instance, if I regret saying something, I would say "I'm sorry" to my higher self and the recipient of my gaffe. Being aware and sorry is the first step in self-healing.

- ✧ **Step 2**: "Please forgive me." (Forgiveness)
  I like to think of this step as asking the Divine in me to forgive myself and bless whomever or whatever I am thinking about in the moment.

- ✧ **Step 3**: "Thank you." (Gratitude)
  Thank yourself, thank God, thank your body, thank whatever strikes your fancy.

- ✧ **Step 4**: "I love you." (Love)
  Say it to anything and everything. Body, breath, God, the home that shelters you. There is nothing more powerful, or needed, than love.

We are all connected to everyone and everything in the universe. Therefore, everything one does as an individual affects the whole. All thoughts, words, images, prayers, blessings, and deeds are listened to by all that is.
—SERGE KAHILI KING (HAWAIIAN KAHUNA)

KNOWING YOU ARE ENOUGH

While preparing for this book, I asked quite a few women to share their strengths with me. Some answered easily and were able to name more than one strength. I was disturbed, however, at how difficult it was for many women to find, let alone articulate, their strengths. Ah so... an example of how thoroughly we've been brainwashed to downplay our own strength and competence. As Rupi Kaur so aptly states, "What is the greatest lesson a woman should learn? That, since day one, she's already had everything she needs within herself. It's the world that convinced her she did not."

A conversation with her sister led Jane to share, "A strength of mine is knowing who I'm *not* and being content with that." I've known Jane since high school and can vouch for about a million of her strengths, and yet it was easier for her to accept what she's not than to acknowledge what she is. Granted, Jane and I are from the "Silent Generation." Thankfully, if our daughters and granddaughters are good examples, we know many younger women are more aware of, and better able to act from, their powerful wisdom and strength.

How about you? Do you fully appreciate yourself and your unique strengths? Do you know you are enough? As is? Right now? Even if you doubt you are enough, you are! As Rumi says, "You were born from the rays of God's majesty when stars were in their perfect place," and Ethel Waters reiterates, "I am somebody 'cause God don't make no junk."

Take a couple of quiet minutes now to close your eyes, and notice your breath moving in and out of your body. Relax. When you feel present, invite an image of yourself to float into your mind's eye. Surround the bodily you and your image with two beautiful, iridescent bubbles of light. Imagine a golden thread connecting your two hearts, and simply enjoy being together. If you find that difficult, invite a loving mother figure into the scene and have her connect you by holding your hands. Very gently allow the image to fade. If you feel drawn to do so, journal about the experience.

When you feel you're not enough—and most of us do, occasionally—give yourself a pat on the back. As Ella Wheeler Wilcox said, "A pat on the back is only a few vertebrae removed from a kick in the pants, but is miles ahead in results." You are enough, just as you are, right here, right now. Please treat yourself accordingly.

During your day...

✧ Gently and regularly affirm and feel your enoughness.

> *The snow goose need not bathe to make itself white.*
> *Neither need you do anything but be yourself.*
>
> —LAO TZU

TREASURING WISDOM

I resonate with the adage "Your best teacher is your last mistake." Since mistakes are inevitable as well as educational, wouldn't it be wise to celebrate rather than condemn them? Mary Bell, my friend and teacher, is great at doing that. A mistake shows up—her own or someone else's—and she lets out a whoop of amusement and joy accompanied by applause or a high-five. Around her, mistakes become treasures leading to a wealth of healing and wisdom.

As the fable goes, a wise mother sends her daughter through a magic portal with the goal of honing her soul by gathering wisdom, kindness, and compassion. The daughter pleads with her mother to be allowed to stay home. But the wise mother insists. The young woman vows, "I will never forget you" and her mother replies, "Ah, yes, you will. And, when the time is right, you will re-remember and return to me carrying treasures beyond your imagination." And off the daughter goes into the unknown questing for soul-growth.

And here you are.

Each day you grow, learn, make mistakes, and gather the treasures they expose. Every now and then a memory of Wholeness and Unconditional Love wafts through your heart, dreams, and maybe even your brain. And then it's back to gleaning kindness, compassion, strength, and wisdom. Each priceless gem is stored in your soul's treasure chest to be shared and celebrated both consciously and unconsciously. Each experience, adventure, and misadventure has within it the opportunity to expand love and open to wisdom. Each experience and every mistake give you the chance to train your head to be of service to your heart and, as a result, return you to your natural state of balance and harmony.

In your mind's eye, imagine a beautiful treasure chest. Admire its craftsmanship and the materials from which it's made. Inside are miniature scrolls attached to small bags holding priceless gifts. Remove one from the chest. The scroll tells the story of an experience, attitude, or mistake that taught you valuable lessons. The bag contains the gifts received from the learning. Jot them down and treasure each one. You earned them, and Mother is proud.

During your day...

- ✧ Treasure wisdom you have gained. Share it generously and graciously.
- ✧ Honor the strength and fortitude it has taken to live the life you were given and know there is endless strength within to call upon.
- ✧ Celebrate mistakes and welcome the treasures they provide.

Keep what is worth keeping, and then, with the breath of kindness, blow the rest away.

—Dinah Craik

REPLENISHING THROUGH CREATIVITY

To function optimally, each aspect of your wondrous self needs rest and replenishment. Without times of renewal, neither muscle, emotion, nor mind or spirit can function well. Since we all know how crucial sleep is for replenishing—and throngs of us still don't get enough—I won't even go there.

Creativity is your daily bread. You get kids ready for school (which, in my experience, required a *lot* of creativity); you balance budgets and schedules—at times a creative miracle; you manage relationships, professions, meals, and countless other responsibilities and recreations. True, there is no shortage of creativity required to simply move life along in a reasonable fashion, but how often do you make time for the pleasure and renewal of *intentional* creativity?

Intentional creativity is a respite for the soul. It is life-enhancing, emotion-healing, and rejuvenating. I can almost hear a few of you saying, "I don't have a creative bone in my body!" Frankly, I don't believe you. You are a woman and, as such, were created to create. My friend Carol, who claims she is not creative, may not be adept at art projects, but she can always figure out how to make disparate bits of confusing text and photographs fit together into a great newsletter. She is also a cat-whisperer with a knack for making people feel welcome. Maybe Carol isn't classically creative, but she is creative nonetheless. As are you.

Creativity is unique to each person. If you lose track of time during any activity (social media and other computerish pastimes may be exceptions), you can bet that's creativity in action. Whether your creativity expresses as gardening, playing/creating music, investing, teaching, knitting, inventing, writing poetry, painting, or performing, for instance, engaging in it replenishes your soul as it balances the hemispheres of your brain.

Creativity is wisdom, love, and joy expressing themselves. Where creativity flows, energy grows.

During your day...

✦ With gentle curiosity, explore your creative interests. When you are completely engrossed in an activity and lose track of time, are you being creative?

✦ Give your left brain a break, and do something fun and creative with your hands. Messy is absolutely okay.

✦ Please enhance your health by getting enough sleep as often as possible. (It's so important, I just couldn't stop myself....)

Balances the brain, Strengthens and replenishes Creativity
—HAIKU BY SUE

SPREADING GENTLE KINDNESS

In the depths of my heart I believe that humankind is basically that—kind and good, heartful rather than hurtful. In light (well, really, *darkness*) of much of the world's inhumanity, it's sometimes hard to maintain a belief in human*kind*, but it is always possible to *be* kind and gentle. The gentleness I am speaking of is strong and powerful, resolute and respectful, as well as wise and relational. A strong, empowered feminine gentleness... former president and CEO of the Global Fund for Women, Kavita Ramdas, succinctly describes gentle kindness as I envision it: "We need women who are so strong they can be gentle, so educated they can be humble, so fierce they can be compassionate, so passionate they can be rational, so disciplined, they can be free."

A compassionate and respectful world begins with us. We are the ones called to bring about change, lighten the darkness, and right inequities. Let us make a commitment to answer the Dalai Lama's appeal to "Be kind whenever possible. It's always possible!" with both attitude and action. Let us embody St. Francis de Sales's philosophy that "Nothing is so strong as gentleness, nothing is so gentle as real strength."

To bring balance and harmony to the forefront of society, may you seed your families, communities, and the world with kindness. Very importantly, may you consistently treat yourself with gentle kindness.

During your day…

- ✧ Be a gentle, kind, and caring friend to yourself and those whose lives you touch.
- ✧ Know the heart-full power of your inborn strength and use it compassionately.

> *Your acts of kindness are iridescent wings of divine love which linger and continue to uplift others long after your sharing.*
>
> —RUMI

12

KNOWING YOU
ARE NOT ALONE

*For beautiful eyes, look for the good in others; for beautiful
lips, speak only words of kindness; and for poise (strength),
walk with the knowledge that you are never alone.*

—AUDREY HEPBURN

Solitude is nurturing, revitalizing, and healing. Isolation is not. When
you can enjoy your own company and have fun playing in the fascinating
vistas of your own mind, solitude feels uplifting and restorative. On the
other hand, if you are alone and struggling with self-esteem or difficult
circumstances like bullying or abuse, loneliness can be debilitating and
dangerous to your health. In my experience, the stronger I become,
the more I am able to enjoy solitude, take steps to safeguard against
isolation, and believe I am never spiritually alone.

The best protection against loneliness and isolation is having
authentic, honest, and supportive relationships with yourself, a circle of
friends and family, and the Divine Beloved in whatever guise resonates

with your soul. All of the topics we've discussed throughout this book help foster those relationships.

As a little kid, I had angels and fairies and God as invisible friends. As an adult, I'm convinced many ethereal helpers and guides are with me whenever I need them and, often, just for the fun of it. On rare occasions, I've actually seen images of angelic presences. Because I've learned to call on them, I feel the presence of my "crew" and other spiritual energies almost daily. My heart knows that, in this universe and beyond, there is much more wonderfulness than I can ever imagine. Many of you can probably see or sense aspects of the Divine in your own unique ways. Such comforting glimpses and goosebumps assure us we are not alone.

CONNECTING WITH THE MYSTERIOUS

From a young age, many of us are naturally connected to the world of spirit. Bobbie is a great example. Born and raised on a Hawaiian sugar plantation, Bobbie had a Japanese nanny. One afternoon when she was three years old sitting on the stoop of her nanny's home waiting for her parents, who were very late, she questioned why she was not included in either her nanny's home or her own. In her words,

Lost in a chasm of loneliness between these two worlds, the anguish of abandonment washed through me. Something mysterious pulled me out of my angst and into a welcoming world that offered me guidance for life. I felt a strong urge to look up and see the sun setting behind the sugar cane fields. The leaves were gently swaying when suddenly a cluster of these leaves came alive and waved directly at me. Next a white ball of information penetrated my being, offering me companionship and comfort along with a message that, in addition to more of the pain I had just experienced, I would have a wonderful life filled with a mission to reach solely for my best self, while inspiring others to do the same.

Having founded a counseling center in Hawaii with Bobbie and been friends for over forty years, I have watched her fulfill her mission as an inspiring teacher, therapist, parenting expert, and advocate for whales and dolphins. We all come into this world firmly connected to and aware of Spirit, but for us, unlike Bobbie, the awareness usually fades as we leave childhood.

A good way to reconnect with mysteries within and without is to hold the *intention* to connect and then *pay attention*. Although mysteries are quiet, subtle, and indirect, they do love relating to us.

During your day...

✧ Find a time when you will not be disturbed. With whatever you prefer writing notes on handy, settle yourself comfortably and close your eyes. Focus on your breathing for a few cycles. In your mind's eye, move back through time to your birth. Welcome your infant self and feel warm and fuzzy toward this precious, brand new being. Do the same with other childhood ages through your teenage years. After you have greeted several of your childhood selves, focus on your breath again for a few cycles. Very gently, with no expectations, ask your inner children if they have anything even slightly mysterious to share with you. If no answers come, that's okay; just continue to be with your "kids" and let them be completely safe with you. Over time, memories or real-time suggestions of the mysterious may arise.

✧ A simpler way to reconnect is to pay close attention to coincidences, as they are often ethereal "hellos."

> *We are meant to be emissaries of the Light*
> *and intermediaries for the Divine.*

VALUING THE LIKE-HEARTED

In a world where the feminine is often denigrated and the genders seem pitted against each other, I wanted to show you that we are not alone. We've gone from men like Napoleon Bonaparte who said, "Women are nothing but machines for producing children" to many—past and present—who see, hear, and support us and the feminine qualities of compassion, equality, and inclusion we embody.

To clarify, my definition of feminist is the same as Gloria Steinem's: "A feminist is anyone who recognizes the equality and full humanity of women and men."

Following are comments from leaders whose words I admire: Justin Trudeau, prime minister of Canada since 2015:

> We shouldn't be afraid of the word "feminist." Men and women should use it to describe themselves.

Barack Obama, president of the United States from 2009 to 2017:

> That's what twenty-first century feminism is about: the idea that when everybody is equal, we are all more free.

Martin Luther King, Jr., minister and equal rights advocate:

> I have a dream that my four little children will one day live in a nation where they will not be judged by the color of their skin, but by the content of their character.

Mahatma Gandhi, leader of the Indian Independence Movement:

> To call woman the weaker sex is a libel; it is man's injustice to woman. If by strength is meant brute strength, then, indeed, is woman less brute than man. If by strength is meant moral power, then woman is immeasurably man's superior.

And my personal favorite...
William Golding, British novelist, playwright, and poet:

> I think women are foolish to pretend they are equal to men. They are far superior and always have been. Whatever you give a woman, she will make greater. If you give her sperm, she will give you a baby. If you give her a house, she will give you a home. If you give her groceries, she will give you a meal. If you give her a smile, she will give you her heart. She multiplies and enlarges what is given to her. So, if you give her any crap, be ready to receive a ton of shit!

During your day…

✦ Notice and appreciate the like-hearted people and circumstances gracing your life.

> *I believe for all our challenges, we live at a glorious moment*
> *in history. It's a moment when, at long last, women have made*
> *it clear that we will no longer be controlled, manipulated,*
> *or abused. I stand with all those women and with those*
> *men equally outraged who support us in heart and mind.*
>
> —JANET JACKSON

BASKING IN NATURE'S REFLECTION

Four years ago a volunteer tulip appeared in our front Zen garden. The first year, she graced us with one red bloom. Each year she's grown and produced different colored flowers. This year, she has a stunning profusion of two whites and fifteen peachy pink blossoms, some with green swirls. I've named her Eve, chuckle at her yearly subpersonalities, and love that she adorns herself according to her mood.

After receiving a picture of Eve's current incarnation, my friend Lea wrote, "OMG! Isn't God/dess wonderful. I think nature like this is supposed to teach us what we are really like on the inside. This beautiful, when we can uncover it."

What a pleasing concept! Is there a tulipness inside me waiting to be discovered? How might a peony reflect the inner musings of my heart? Is there an internal giant Sequoia I can lean on? If it appeals to you, entertain the idea of a favorite flower being a reflection of a unique talent or yearning of yours. Contemplating how your essence may be reflected in nature's awesome complexity feels like a playfully profound way to relate with our rich environment and an absolute affirmation that we are watched over and delighted in by a loving and benign Creatress.

Allow the inspiration of Mother Nature to grace your life. From the tiniest seed to the tallest tree, she has enchantments to share with your heart and soul. Spending a few minutes mindfully and gratefully observing nature is amazingly uplifting. If going outside is impossible, or nature is mostly concreted over where you are, appreciate a houseplant or pet. When no living nature is within reach, magazines, television, or the internet can provide beautiful images to peruse. No matter how you connect with her, Mother Nature is a spa day for the soul.

As well as being an invaluable spiritual mentor and reflection of our inner beauty, nature is also the Beloved's unceasing assurance of, "Hi Honey, I'm here!" Enjoy nature, be enthralled by her loveliness, and be inspired to blossom in your own special way.

During your day...

✦ Devote five minutes or more to enjoying a beautiful or delightful aspect of nature.

✦ Muse on the qualities you enjoy in nature. Might they be reflecting your own?

✦ Mindfully notice and appreciate beauty, wherever and whatever it is.

Mother Nature's beauty and grandeur mirror your own.

FILLING UP AND OVERFLOWING

To me, the natural phenomenon of daybreak clearly points out we are not alone. Whether we see it or not, sunrise happens each morning and light returns. Each day God gives us the incredible gift of light, free of charge. Blessed by this amazing resource, we can discern obstacles, move easily, see and be seen clearly, accomplish things that would be impossible without illumination, warm ourselves, and soak up vitamin D.

Just knowing light will return gives us comfort and support when we are experiencing darkness of all kinds. As women, we confront darkness with powerful strength. As a result, we are often called upon to do so not only for ourselves but also for others who need our wisdom and stability.

We are adept at handling inner and outer darkness as well as physical, emotional, mental, and spiritual darkness. However, because we are human, such responsibility can be depleting unless we mindfully refill our energetic chalices on a regular basis. It's important to ascertain what fills your heart to overflowing and replenish yourself by making time for it. It's wise to nourish ourselves by inviting the gift of Light to fill and flow through us for the well-being of all.

Smiles are light flowing from us to others. Studies show that the act of smiling physically lifts our spirits. Giving a smile to someone else may be just what they need in that moment to lighten their heart. We can emulate the sweet-hearted teacher Paramahansa Yogananda, who said, "Let my soul smile through my heart and my heart smile through my eyes, that I may scatter rich smiles in sad hearts."

Light, and the love it symbolizes, is a promise we can take to heart, a gift that is here to stay.

During your day…

- ✧ Be aware of sunlight or candlelight. Invite it to fill you to overflowing. Bask in feelings of warmth and well-being.
- ✧ Take tender care of yourself as you care for others.
- ✧ Scatter rich smiles….

Light is the element that clears out old distortions
and allows you to see through the lens of Love.

—BELINDA PEARL

ASKING FOR HELP

Have you ever had one of those days when you screw up one thing after another and feel terrible as a result? Earlier this year, I did. Mercifully, I can't remember the details, but for some reason Gene was unhappy and I had fallen into an old pattern of taking responsibility for "making him unhappy." So, I felt badly about that and, probably at a deeper level, was also ticked off at myself for reverting to old behavior. On top of that, I screwed up by thoughtlessly telling one of my kids something that had the possibility of hurting their feelings.

After that phone call, I was so upset I felt nauseous and couldn't "pardon" myself no matter what I tried. In fact, I didn't even have the energy to do one of the exercises that usually helps me when I'm emotionally bereft. I still felt like a really *bad* person at bedtime. To comfort myself while I tried to sleep, I held a special rose quartz angel my daughter-in-love gave me in one hand and a little teddy bear that is meaningful to me in the other. And I begged God, my guardian and guideian angels, and whoever or whatever was wherever to help me while I slept.

Around four o'clock I woke up from a vivid dream. The main character was an Indiana Jones type fellow, and the setting was a war zone. Even though dangerously under fire, Indiana deftly managed to get many people to safety. Among those he rescued were orphans with wings, politically and racially persecuted men and women, a friend of mine who was abused as a child, and several of her support group friends. A short ceasefire was called in order to acknowledge and praise the heroes. The Indiana type hero, whom I had both witnessed and been in the dream, was named Chris Divinity. Right after his name was shouted through a public address system, I woke up. It wasn't until I was writing down the dream that I got it. Chris Divinity! I love it when the spiritual realm shows its humorous side.

Although I'm not an expert in dream analysis, I gleaned several benefits from this one. First, I felt better. Second, the name made me chuckle aloud, and laughter is a healing balm to me. Third, and very importantly, I felt heard, reassured, and held. Because I'd played the part of Chris Divinity as well as being an observer of him, I received the twofold message: "I've got your back" and "You've had others' backs." I had literally called out of the darkness for help and received it.

During your day...

⬥ Give yourself the loving gift of asking for help. Our angels and helper beings want to be of service but must be asked before they can do so.

For every soul there is a guardian watching it.
—KORAN, 86:4

CULTIVATING AN INNER ADVOCATE

Even though human and heavenly assistance is available, the most crucial help we need remains our own. One of the most supportive and strengthening things you can do for yourself is cultivate an inner advocate who believes in your goodness, worthiness, and wisdom. An inner advocate is an ambassador from your heart—an aspect of yourself who admires, respects, and adores you.

An inner advocate radiates acceptance; is curious, but not judgmental; interested, but not overly attached; adoring, but not sentimental; wise, but not preachy; supportive, but not enabling. She is a steadfast, loving, and understanding friend.

My inner advocate has evolved into a combination of the therapist I was, my adult self, and a red-headed angel, who appeared to me in a dental office. She is always level-headed, understanding, and open-hearted. My advocate's name is Sam because she feels sweet, adoring, and mischievous to me. Sam usually calls me Susie, my childhood nickname, which is perfect since she has become my inner ideal mother and friend.

As a visual person, I feel comfortable relating to Sam by picturing her. But we are all different, so your inner advocate will be uniquely yours. For instance, you may relate to the *concept* of an accepting inner voice and hear what it shares, or it may be satisfying to use a journal and dialog with your advocate. A friend of mine thinks of hers as the *still small voice within.* It doesn't matter how you experience your loving, gentle, and wise inner friend. It's only important that you do.

If cultivating an inner advocate appeals to you, close your eyes and place your attention on the sounds around you. As you focus on the sounds, call back any energy that is lingering around today's previous activities. Gently welcome dispersed energy back to your body and this moment. When you feel gathered together, turn your attention to your breath and allow it to breathe you for a few moments. Imagine yourself in a safe and beautiful environment, an actual place or a creation of your imagination. Make yourself comfortable and enjoy what you see, hear, and feel in this beautiful setting. Intuitively, you know your inner advocate is near. Invite it to make itself known to you in ways that resonate with your soul. Be present and allow yourself to sense, see, know, or hear your advocate. If you have questions, ask and open to responses. Thank your inner advocate whether you are connected or not. It may take a few invitations to begin cultivating a relationship.

During your day…

✧ Cultivate a deep and loyal friendship with yourself.

> *Sure you can be your own worst enemy, but you can also be your own best friend. You are never truly alone when you learn to completely fall in love with your soul.*
>
> —MELANIE JOY

PRACTICING FAIR FIERCENESS

I love the adage "Coincidences are God's way of remaining anonymous." Since angels are said to be God's messengers, I like to see coincidences as angelic hellos. This morning's angelic message was especially welcome because I've been in the midst of a frustrating, deadline-threatening writer's block and was in need of an obvious attagirl.

Between feeding the dog and helping Gene with a little chore, I was scratching out a few sticky notes when my phone dinged, alerting me to the word of the day. Because, at that very moment, I was trying to figure out which word combination—*fair fierceness* or *fierce fairness*—best fit an attitude women needed to adopt, the word of the day leaped out at me. *Objurgate: rebuke severely; scold; to reproach or denounce vehemently; upbraid harshly; berate sharply.* I laughed. Okay, fair fierceness, it is.

Granted, as defined above, objurgating behavior is too over the top, much more masculine than feminine in nature and, therefore, less effective in getting us where we want to go. But it was still a great attagirl! A mama bear message underscoring the need for me—and you—to bring our power forward with fair fierceness. In our quest for balance and equality, the definition of fierceness I choose is "heartfelt and powerful intensity."

Yesterday, my daughter Paige told me a story that exemplifies heartfelt and powerful intensity. During the 2016 Women's March in Washington, DC, Paige was among a multitude of people passionately chanting about love and fairness on the steps of the Lincoln Memorial.

Notable women's rights attorney Gloria Allred was close by as were several anti-rights men wearing "Fear the Lord" and "Women Belong in the Kitchen" T-shirts and shouting dire hellfire and brimstone warnings. Gloria Allred put her arm around a preteen girl in the crowd saying, "We need more girls like you!" and the two of them walked up to the men. With heartfelt and powerful intensity, Gloria said, "You don't belong here. You need to leave." And they did.

During your day…

- ✧ View coincidences as sweet angelic encouragements.
- ✧ Muse about areas in your life that might benefit from heartfelt, powerful, and intense fair fierceness.

> *Angelic attagirls are always positive and*
> *often spiked with sassy, sweet humor.*
> *Fair fierceness can be the same.*

GAINING STRENGTH FROM SILENCE AND SOLITUDE

> *There is the in-breath and there is the out-breath, and*
> *it's easy to believe that we must exhale all the time,*
> *without ever inhaling. But the inhale is absolutely*
> *essential if you want to continue to exhale.*
>
> —ROSHI JOAN HALIFAX

We live in an out-breath society, an out-of-balance culture valuing outward expression, busyness, and extensive doingness above taking the time to breathe in, muse, and come to know ourselves wholly. Physical, emotional, and spiritual well-being require a balance of in and out, give and take, and expression and contemplation. In silence and solitude, we touch our essence, connect with our core divinity, and are attentive to the whispers of our souls. A rested, centered soul arises from the soft safety of quietly being in our own feminine presence. True strength has the courage to outwardly express inner authenticity.

In silence and solitude, strength wraps her mighty arms around you and claims you as her own. In the arms of strength, your authentic Self is free to share her wisdom and open your eyes to the reservoir of courage and integrity at the core of your being. In silence and solitude, Spirit welcomes you home.

Okay, if solitude and silence are so darn fulfilling, why don't we *do* it more often? I don't know about you, but before I got hooked on my daily medi-play/medi-pray times, I would get swept up in all the things I wanted and needed to do and forget how much I loved solitude and silence. I forgot, as May Sarton promises, that "Solitude is the salt of personhood. It brings out the authentic flavor of every experience." In a fog of forgetfulness, it's so easy to succumb to the seduction of *doing* and ignore the quiet call of your soul.

Of course, time and circumstances are huge factors in how much silence and solitude you can get and still sleep. In my season of life, opportunities abound. But, if you are responsibility-swamped right now, silence and solitude may be elusive and require creative planning to manage. I remember how hard that is and, even so, hope you can find time to rest in the sanctuary of your own presence.

During your day…

- ✧ Ask yourself what strengths may be waiting in the silence for you to discover.
- ✧ (You can do this little meditation practice anywhere— sitting at a stoplight, waiting in the school pickup line, staring at a computer screen, wherever….) As you inhale, breathe in something you want or need from the universe. As you exhale, breathe out something positive for someone else. For instance, today I am breathing in enough time and creativity to finish this book by its looming deadline, and I'm breathing out peace of mind and health for a friend with a scary diagnosis.

> *May the water of your soul be still enough*
> *to reflect back your truest self.*
> —Augusta Kantra

NOTICING ANGELS EVERYWHERE

Evidence of angelic presence is reassuring in a world that seems to be running amuck. Hope, trust, and strength are easier to maintain when we choose to concentrate on beauty, kindness, and angelic autographs rather than negativity. Once we decide to be aware of them, angels have fun getting our attention. Like us, they seem to enjoy being recognized and appreciated. Plus, it's an angel's job and joy to guide, protect, and love you unconditionally. My intuition assures me angels actually delight in us; that our antics and, yes, even our naiveté/ignorance amuse and endear us to them.

You probably have your own ways of knowing when your angels and helper beings are saying, "Hi, I'm here." Two external signs that alert me to ethereal hellos are (1) finding heart shapes—in potato chips, cactus pods, rocks, oil stains, dog food, TP rolls, broccoli, clouds… and (2) when a casual glance at a digital clock shows consecutive or similar numbers, such as 11:11, 1:23, 5:55. One day, when I was terribly worried about one of my kids, I "accidentally" saw 11:11, 2:22, 2:34, 3:33, and 3:45 and felt better as a result. My daughter Paige finds feathers even in very nonfeathery places. The main internal signal that divine energy is with me is a tingly sensation starting between my shoulder blades (or "wings," it just occurred to me!) going up through my neck and cupping my skull. A wash of gratitude and awe usually accompanies the tingles. A full-blown idea breezing through my mind also feels like angelic assistance.

The most unusual angelic reassurance I ever received was meeting a doppelgänger of my spiritual mother, Annabelle, on the path behind our house. At the very moment I was asking for angelic help leading an upcoming women's retreat, there she was walking toward me. *My* Annabelle, who'd been dead for three years. Literally, a dead ringer. I had never seen the real-life woman before, nor have I seen her since. But I got the message loud and clear.

During your day...

⋄ Ask your angels to help you be aware of their presence.
⋄ Bask in angelic love and listen for caring guidance.
⋄ Tune your heart and mind to physical, emotional, and intuitive signs signaling the presence of benevolent energy of all kinds.

> *Go forth with confidence and go forth in peace. For there are angels to your left and angels to your right; angels in front of you and angels behind you; angels above you and angels below. You are loved, and you are not alone.*
>
> —MARIANNE WILLIAMSON

ADDING VALUE

In response to my thank you for his help to Gene and me during a crisis, our son answered, "Several years ago, I decided to try and add value to any situation I'm in or person I'm with." Wow. I like that so much more than *being of service*. For some reason, the concept of service makes me uneasy. To me, it hints at a one up/one down dynamic, while *adding value* feels egalitarian, doable, and a great way to make a positive difference. It's probably just a semantic issue, but adding value feels right to me, and the idea has been a life-enhancing lesson for me.

Michelle Obama's idea "Success isn't about how much money you make; it's about the difference you make in people's lives" resonates with me. We can make a difference and add value to people's lives in tiny ways. A supportive or congratulatory text, email, or phone call can make a difference to someone who feels alone. Remembering birthdays or other special occasions adds value to celebrations large and small. Being available to listen, console, or commiserate can help soothe an aching heart and, by being heard, make its person feel seen and valued.

Each of us is a work in progress, divinity clothed in a garment of flesh—sort of like a corndog, provided you think corndogs are heavenly. Which I do, on occasion. No matter how corny and crusty our outer shells may appear, there remains within us the treasure of an unblemished soul longing to add value to our own lives and the lives of our brothers and sisters. Each of us has treasures to share that can make a difference to those receiving them. A generous tip, a sincere compliment, an anonymous scholarship, an understanding heart, donating a kidney, holding a hand, or giving a hug—all add value. It is your basic nature to give, to comfort, to include, and to share in tiny and tremendous ways. Your soul's desire is to meaningfully connect, love yourself and others, and make a difference in our beautiful and beleaguered world.

During your day...

✦ Add value to your life in ways that make your soul sing.

✦ Add value to each situation you're in and person you're with.

✦ A point to remember: When you are receiving treasure from others, 98.7 percent of the time, giving it expands their heart and, thereby, adds value to their life.

> *We are all born with a divine fire in us. Our efforts should be to give wings to this fire and fill the world with the glow of its goodness.*
>
> —ABDUL KALAM

CREATING A GROUNDING CORD

Even though it's wonderful to know you have guides and protectors in the angelic realm, your most indispensable guardian angel is yourself. It's up to you to choose to be a protective, supportive, and loving forever-friend to yourself. We are our sole constants throughout lifetimes, the *me, myself,* and *I*'s always present, so we darn well better have our own backs!

One of the best "back-having" practices I've learned is creating a grounding cord. We touched on them briefly in the meditation "Lighting Up and Letting Flow" in chapter 5. To explore further, grounding cords are similar to the tap roots fruits and vegetables use to anchor themselves in the soil. Like tap roots, grounding cords are strong and stabilizing, but unlike tap roots, grounding cords are used to release, let go of, and flush out energy rather than absorb and take in nutrients.

Take a few quiet minutes now in which to create your own personal grounding cord. Get comfy and allow your eyes to drift shut. Gently turn your attention to your breath and simply experience it for a few cycles. No hurry, no effort. Say a sweet hello to your body, thanking it for making it possible for you to exist in this time and form. Allow awareness to move to the base of your spine and imagine a grounding cord as wide as your hips gently sinking toward the center of Mother Earth. My grounding cord often resembles a tree trunk, Lee's is a sparkling column of light, Pat's is a trash shoot, and kids often have monkey tails. Whatever you see is fine as long as it feels right to you.

Just for fun, grounding cords often change how they look. When your cord reaches the center of the Earth, imagine a place for it to secure itself. Anchor it there. Effortlessly invite unwanted energy stored in your body to flow down the grounding cord to be transformed and transmuted in the heart of the Mother.

I've been doing the grounding cord practice daily for over a year. As a result, I feel stronger, less swayed by winds of change or whiffs of criticism. I feel safer and, consequently, more loved and protected. I am more balanced and earthy, yet better able to access the magical and mysterious. I feel cleaner and clearer.

During your day…

⬧ Freshen up your grounding cord whenever you think of it and clear and cleanse your body by releasing unwanted energy.

⬧ If someone you love is ill or out of sorts, ground them.

⬧ Ground your car when on the road.

> *A grounding cord is an energy connection from the base of the spine to the center of the earth. It allows you to release unwanted energies from the body. As we ground, room is created for our spiritual essence to fully inhabit the body.*
>
> —MARY BELL NYMAN

HANGIN' WITH THE HOLIES

A caveat: This meditation roams the outskirts of my esoteric musings. It's a little weird, but please know these reflections come from an increasingly peaceful and empowered heart.

For eons, mystics, poets, and wise ones have embraced the idea that life is a school, a place of learning and growing, an opportunity to master the art of unconditional love and acceptance. A great school, but not our true Home.

Even though I haven't mastered those lessons, as I get older and meander closer to the Pearly Gates, I am feeling a little homesick. Not that I plan to shuffle off Shakespeare's mortal coil anytime soon, but I can feel myself preparing, which seems chronologically appropriate. Maybe, in converse order to the natural forgetting of Home, I'm intuitively remembering. Perhaps the veil between realms is becoming more translucent, or possibly, it's because I've been hanging out with the holies regularly.

Although it feels incredibly vulnerable to be doing so, I want to share my holies with you. Since my childhood, Jesus has been a friend and brother. Mary, his mother, is also my dear one. As mentioned earlier, about twenty years ago, an angel named Sam (sweet, adoring, and mischievous) appeared to me in the dentist's office. In 1997, on the island of Bimini I found out my forty-nine-year-old sister had died. That afternoon a dolphin swam a long distance to meet me and escort me back to the boat where my sons waited. I named her Auntie Es and had several more awe-inspiring swims with her over the next twenty years. To me, Auntie Es is an angel with fins, and I am teary-eyed writing about her. Following surgery four years ago, I was waiting for anesthetic-induced nausea to pass when I thought someone turned on the light. Prying my eyes open a tiny bit, I saw a brilliant column of light on the right side of the bed. It dissipated, leaving an aura of love and healing behind. His name is Toux. A couple of years ago, during a very scary time in a different hospital, Stormy, a towering Storm Trooper, appeared, and I felt protected. A few weeks ago, my mother sashayed into my semi-circle of Holies, plunked herself between Jesus and Mary, and has been with us ever since. In life, Mother was stoic; in this different life, she is a spunky hoot.

This disparate group makes up the angelic Crew of Holies with whom I hang out.

During your day...

⋄ We all have our personal holies. If you haven't already, do yourself the life-enhancing kindness of befriending your unique Circle of Holies.

May you be well. May you be peaceful.
May you be filled with strength and wisdom.
May you know how much you are loved and love
exactly who you are. May you be love.

ACKNOWLEDGMENTS

Surprised and delighted thanks to publisher, Michael Kerber, whose casual question, "Want to write another book?" reignited a fire I thought long cooled. Applause and a thousand thank yous to Greg Brandenburgh whose editorial expertise is exceeded only by his ability to entertain. Thank you, Greg, for insightful guidance and many chuckles. Gobs of gratitude to production editor, Jane Hagaman, whose easygoing and helpful manner is balm to my writer's soul. Equal dollops of respect and gratitude to Chuck Hutchinson for his copyediting finesse and thoughtful comments accompanying changes. To all the talented people at Conari—many of whom I will never know—whose combined skill and energy crafted this beautiful book, please know I am incredibly appreciative of your efforts on Strength's behalf.

As always, appreciation and gratitude to my husband, Gene, whose encouragement and support helped launch my writing career and keeps the business end of it afloat to this day.

Everlasting gratitude to the *incredible* women everywhere whose powerful hearts create a Sisterhood of Strength.

ABOUT THE AUTHOR

Sue Patton Thoele is the author of numerous books, including *The Courage to Be Yourself* and *The Woman's Book of Courage*. She is a mother, stepmother, grandmother, former psychotherapist, and hospice chaplain. Sue and her husband Gene live in Colorado.

Mango Publishing, established in 2014, publishes an eclectic list of books by diverse authors—both new and established voices—on topics ranging from business, personal growth, women's empowerment, LGBTQ studies, health, and spirituality to history, popular culture, time management, decluttering, lifestyle, mental wellness, aging, and sustainable living. We were recently named 2019 and 2020's #1 fastest-growing independent publisher by *Publishers Weekly*. Our success is driven by our main goal, which is to publish high-quality books that will entertain readers as well as make a positive difference in their lives.

Our readers are our most important resource; we value your input, suggestions, and ideas. We'd love to hear from you—after all, we are publishing books for you!

Please stay in touch with us and follow us at:

Facebook: Mango Publishing
Twitter: @MangoPublishing
Instagram: @MangoPublishing
LinkedIn: Mango Publishing
Pinterest: Mango Publishing
Newsletter: mangopublishinggroup.com/newsletter

Join us on Mango's journey to reinvent publishing, one book at a time.